P9-CRI-540

dition

triumphlearning™
Common Core Coach
Mathematics 3

Dr. Jerry Kaplan
Senior Mathematics Consultant

Common Core Coach, Mathematics, First Edition, Grade 3   T114NA   ISBN-13: 978-1-61997-436-4
Contributing Writers: Andie Liao   **Cover Design:** Q2A/Bill Smith   **Cover Illustration:** Shaw Nielson

Triumph Learning® 136 Madison Avenue, 7th Floor, New York, NY 10016 © 2013 Triumph Learning, LLC. Buckle Down and Coach are imprints of
Triumph Learning. All rights reserved. No part of this publication may be reproduced in whole or in part, stored in a retrieval system, or transmitted in any form
or by any means, electronic, mechanical, photocopying, recording or otherwise, without written permission from the publisher.

Printed in the United States of America.   10 9 8 7 6 5 4 3 2 1

The National Governors Association Center for Best Practices and Council of Chief State School Officers are the sole owners and developers of the Common
Core State Standards, © Copyright 2010. All rights reserved.

Contents

Problem
Solving

Fluency
Lesson

Performance
Task

Grade 2

Grade 3

Grade 4

Grade 2 OA

Represent and solve problems involving addition and subtraction.

Work with equal groups of objects to gain foundations for multiplication.

Grade 3 OA

Represent and solve problems involving multiplication and division.

Understand properties of multiplication and the relationship between multiplication and division.

Multiply and divide within 100.

Solve problems involving the four operations, and identify and explain patterns in arithmetic.

Grade 4 OA

Use the four operations with whole numbers to solve problems.

Gain familiarity with factors and multiples.

Generate and analyze patterns.

Grade 4 NBT

Use place value understanding and properties of operations to perform multi-digit arithmetic.

Grade 2 NBT

Understand place value.

Use place value understanding and properties of operations to add and subtract.

Grade 4 MD

Solve problems involving measurement and conversion of measurements from a larger unit to a smaller unit.

Domain 1
Operations and Algebraic Thinking

1 Representing Multiplication

UNDERSTAND Use models to show **multiplication**.

Show 3×5 as 3 groups of 5 objects. Find the total number of objects.

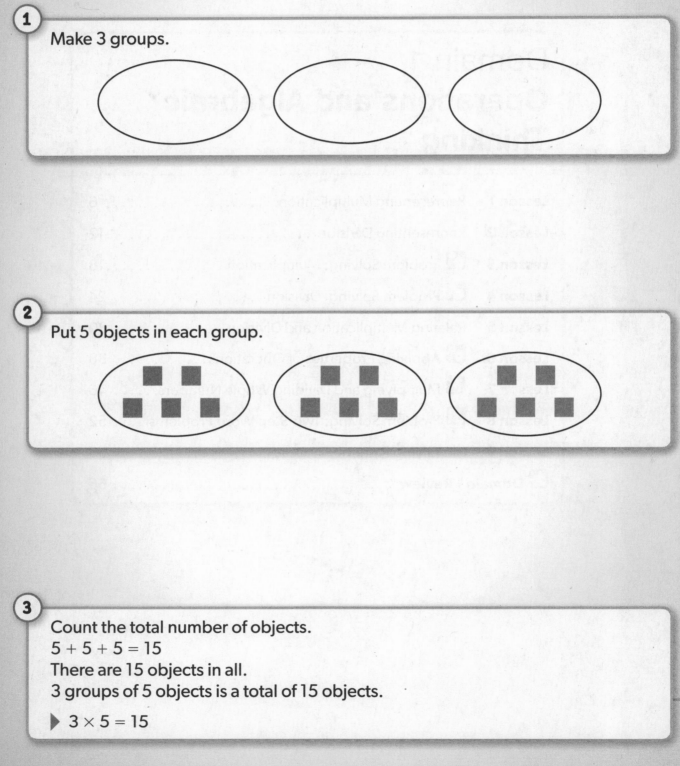

1 Make 3 groups.

2 Put 5 objects in each group.

3 Count the total number of objects.
$5 + 5 + 5 = 15$
There are 15 objects in all.
3 groups of 5 objects is a total of 15 objects.

▶ $3 \times 5 = 15$

Connect

Multiply. 3 × 5

1 Find how many groups there are.

The first **factor** is 3.

There are 3 equal groups.

2 Find how many are in each group.

The second factor is 5.

There are 5 in each group.

3 Find the **product**.

Skip count by 5. Skip count three times.

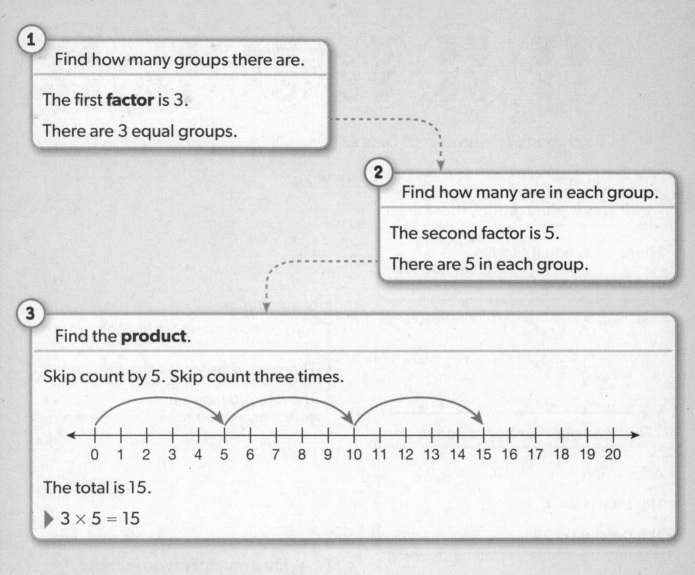

The total is 15.

▶ 3 × 5 = 15

TRY Use skip counting to multiply 3 × 4.

EXAMPLE Jeff has these counting bears.

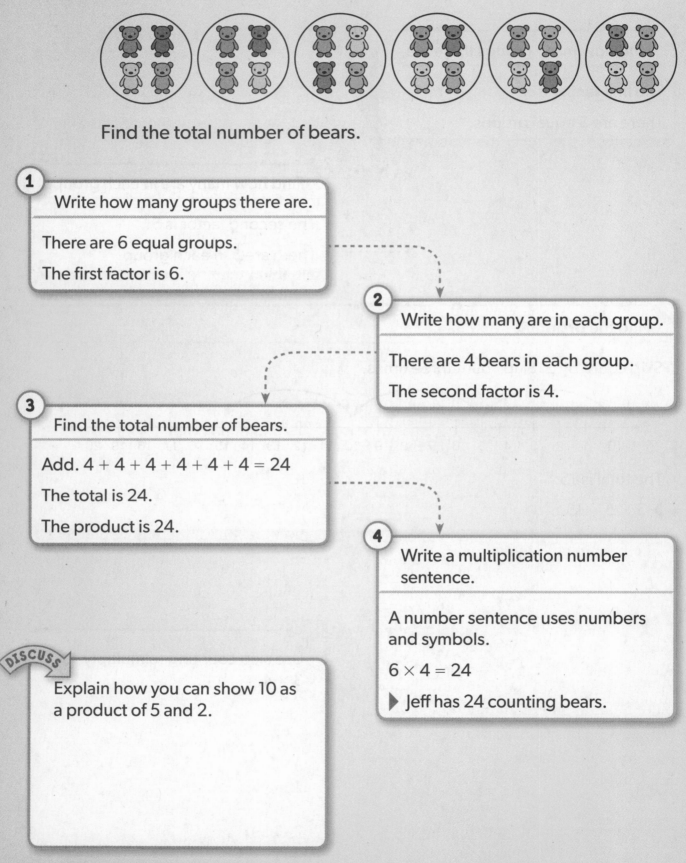

Find the total number of bears.

1 Write how many groups there are.

There are 6 equal groups.

The first factor is 6.

2 Write how many are in each group.

There are 4 bears in each group.

The second factor is 4.

3 Find the total number of bears.

Add. 4 + 4 + 4 + 4 + 4 + 4 = 24

The total is 24.

The product is 24.

4 Write a multiplication number sentence.

A number sentence uses numbers and symbols.

6 × 4 = 24

▶ Jeff has 24 counting bears.

DISCUSS

Explain how you can show 10 as a product of 5 and 2.

Multiplication Models

Draw objects in each group to show the multiplication. Write the total.

1. $2 \times 6 =$ _____

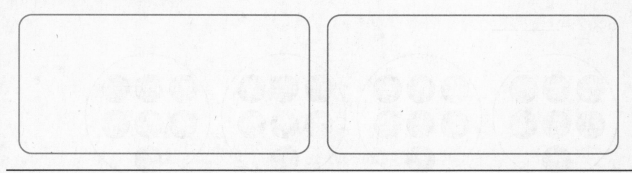

_____

2. $4 \times 3 =$ _____

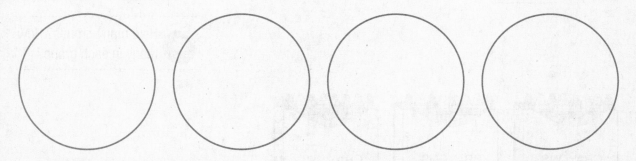

_____

3. $3 \times 7 =$ _____

_____

4. $5 \times 3 =$ _____

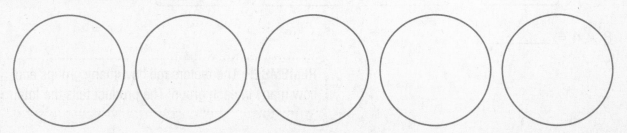

Practice

Fill in the missing numbers to match the picture.

1.
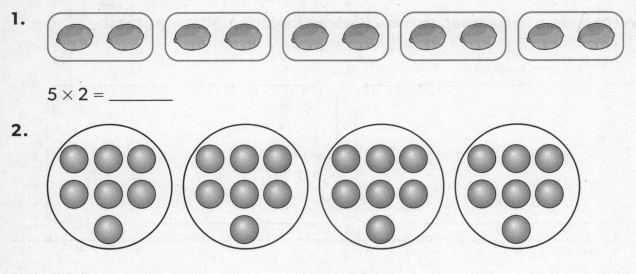

$5 \times 2 =$ _____

2.
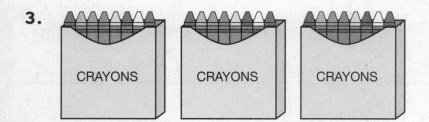

$4 \times 7 =$ _____

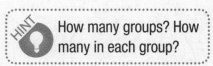
HINT How many groups? How many in each group?

3.
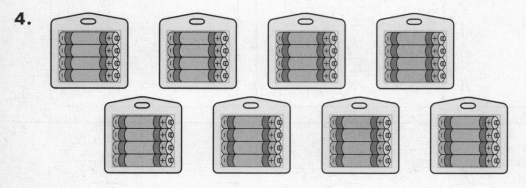

CRAYONS   CRAYONS   CRAYONS

$3 \times 8 =$ _____

4.

$8 \times 4 =$ _____

REMEMBER The factors tell how many groups and how many in each group. The product tells the total.

How many in all? Write a multiplication number sentence.

5. How many wheels in all?

_____ × _____ = _____   _____ wheels

6. How many grapes in all?

_____ × _____ = _____   _____ grapes

Solve.

7. The students are in 5 groups. Each group has 4 students. How many students are there in all?

_____

8. Katie has 4 bags of oranges. Each bag has 8 oranges. How many oranges does Katie have?

_____

9. EXPLAIN What does the multiplication fact $2 \times 6 = 12$ mean?

_____

_____

_____

10. DRAW Show that $7 \times 2 = 14$ by drawing a picture.

2 Representing Division

UNDERSTAND Use models to show **division**.

Divide 12 objects into equal groups. Put 4 objects in each group. How many equal groups are there?

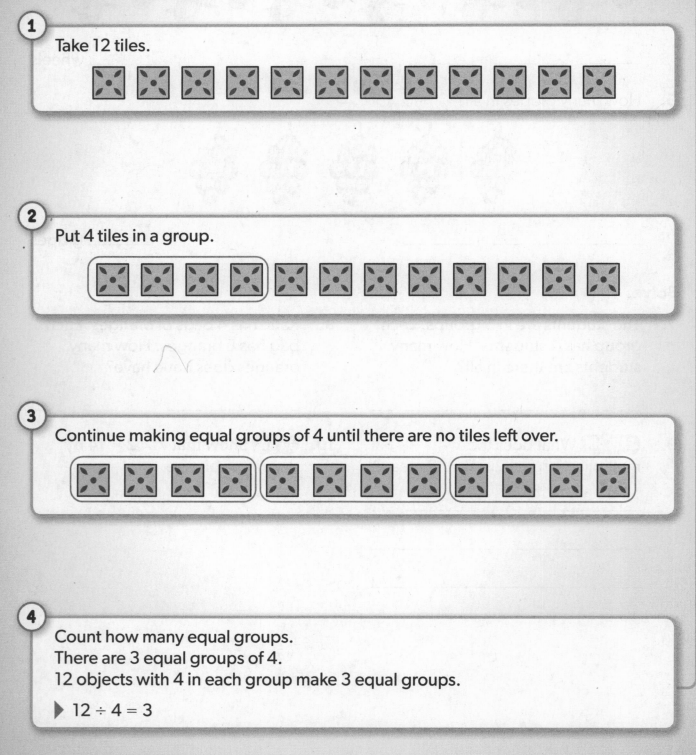

1 Take 12 tiles.

2 Put 4 tiles in a group.

3 Continue making equal groups of 4 until there are no tiles left over.

4
Count how many equal groups.
There are 3 equal groups of 4.
12 objects with 4 in each group make 3 equal groups.

▶ 12 ÷ 4 = 3

⊏ Connect

Divide. 12 ÷ 4

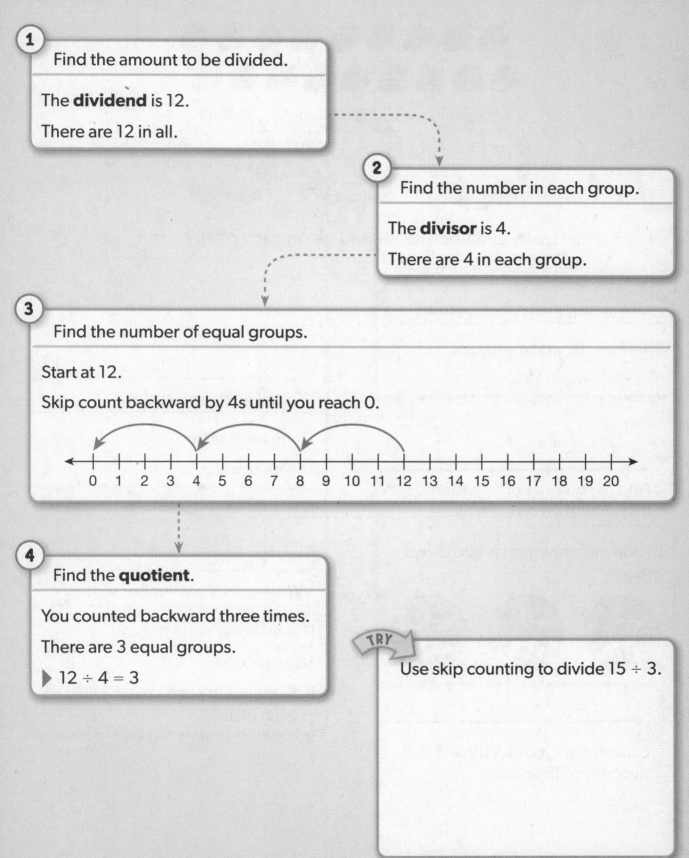

1 Find the amount to be divided.

The **dividend** is 12.

There are 12 in all.

2 Find the number in each group.

The **divisor** is 4.

There are 4 in each group.

3 Find the number of equal groups.

Start at 12.

Skip count backward by 4s until you reach 0.

0 1 2 3 4 5 6 7 8 9 10 11 12 13 14 15 16 17 18 19 20

4 Find the **quotient**.

You counted backward three times.

There are 3 equal groups.

▶ 12 ÷ 4 = 3

TRY

Use skip counting to divide 15 ÷ 3.

EXAMPLE Sam wants to put the same number of strawberries on each plate.

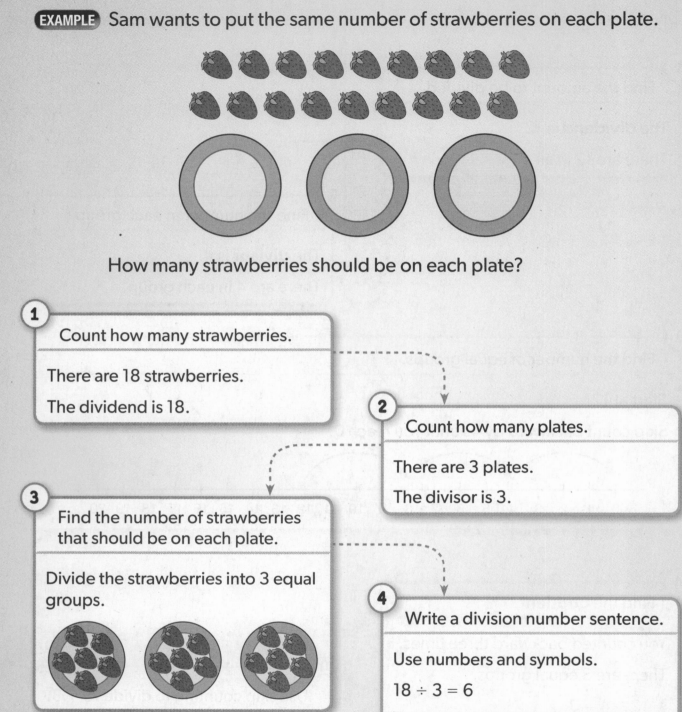

How many strawberries should be on each plate?

1
Count how many strawberries.

There are 18 strawberries.

The dividend is 18.

2
Count how many plates.

There are 3 plates.

The divisor is 3.

3
Find the number of strawberries that should be on each plate.

Divide the strawberries into 3 equal groups.

4
Write a division number sentence.

Use numbers and symbols.

$18 \div 3 = 6$

▶ Sam should put 6 strawberries on each plate.

DISCUSS
Explain how you can show 3 as a quotient of 15 and 5.

Division Models

Use the divisor as the number in each group. Circle the objects. Write how many equal groups.

1. 20 ÷ 4 = _____

_____

2. 28 ÷ 7 = _____

Use the divisor as the number of equal groups. Circle the objects. Write how many in each group.

3. 14 ÷ 2 = _____

_____

4. 24 ÷ 8 = _____

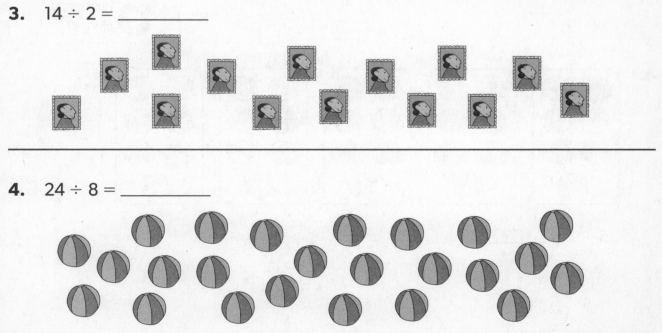

Practice

Fill in the missing number to match each picture.

1.
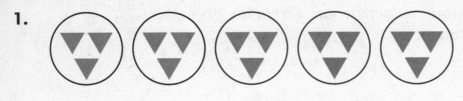

$15 \div 5 =$ _____

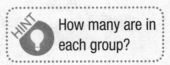 **HINT** How many are in each group?

2.

$24 \div 4 =$ _____

3.
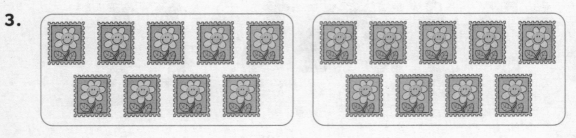

$18 \div 9 =$ _____

HINT How many groups?

4.

$35 \div 7 =$ _____

Write a division number sentence.

5. How many eggs are in each group?

48 ÷ _____ = _____   _____ eggs in each group

6. How many groups of books?

18 ÷ _____ = _____   _____ equal groups

Solve.

7. Five friends share 20 marbles equally. How many marbles will each friend get?

_____

8. Mike wants to put 28 photos in his album. Each page will have 4 photos. How many pages will he fill with his photos?

_____

9. **EXPLAIN** What does the division fact 30 ÷ 5 = 6 mean?

_____

_____

_____

10. **DRAW** Show that 16 ÷ 2 = 8 by drawing a picture.

LESSON 3

Problem Solving: Multiplication

The Cabbage Patch

READ

The cabbages are planted in 4 rows. Each row has 8 heads of cabbage. How many heads of cabbage are there in all?

PLAN

Make an **array** to write an **equation**.

Make 4 equal rows of 8 heads of cabbage.

Let □ = how many heads of cabbage in all

$4 \times 8 = □$

SOLVE

Find the total number in the array.

4 rows of 8 equal _____.

_____ × _____ = _____

CHECK

Use **repeated addition**.

Add 8 four times.

_____ + _____ + _____ + _____ = _____

The product, □, is _____.

▶ There are _____ heads of cabbage in all.

Apple Picking

READ

Casey picked apples at the farm. He put the apples into 5 bowls. Each bowl has 4 apples in it. How many apples does Casey have in all?

PLAN

Draw a picture to write an equation.

Make 5 equal groups with 4 apples in each group.

Let □ = how many apples in all

$5 \times 4 = $ □

SOLVE

Find the total number of apples.

5 groups of 4 equal _____.

_____ × _____ = _____

CHECK

Use repeated addition.

Add 4 five times.

_____ + _____ + _____ + _____ + _____ = _____

The product, □, is _____.

▶ Casey has _____ apples in all.

Weighing Melons

READ

Dana wants to buy 5 melons. Each melon weighs 3 pounds. How many pounds of melons will Dana buy in all?

PLAN

Draw a picture to write an equation.

Draw 5 melons. Each melon is 3 pounds.

3 pounds   3 pounds   3 pounds   3 pounds   3 pounds

Let □ = how many pounds in all

5 × 3 = □

SOLVE

Find the total weight of the melons.

Use repeated addition.

Add 3 five times.

3 + 3 + 3 + 3 + 3 = 15

5 groups of 3 equal _____.

_____ × _____ = _____

CHECK

Use skip counting.

Skip count by 3s five times.

_____, _____, _____, _____, _____

The product, □, is _____.

▶ Dana will buy _____ pounds of melons in all.

Woodworking

READ

Chris has a board that is 2 feet long. He has another board that is 4 times as long. How long is the second board?

PLAN

Draw a picture to write an equation.

One board is 2 feet long. The other board is 4 times as long.

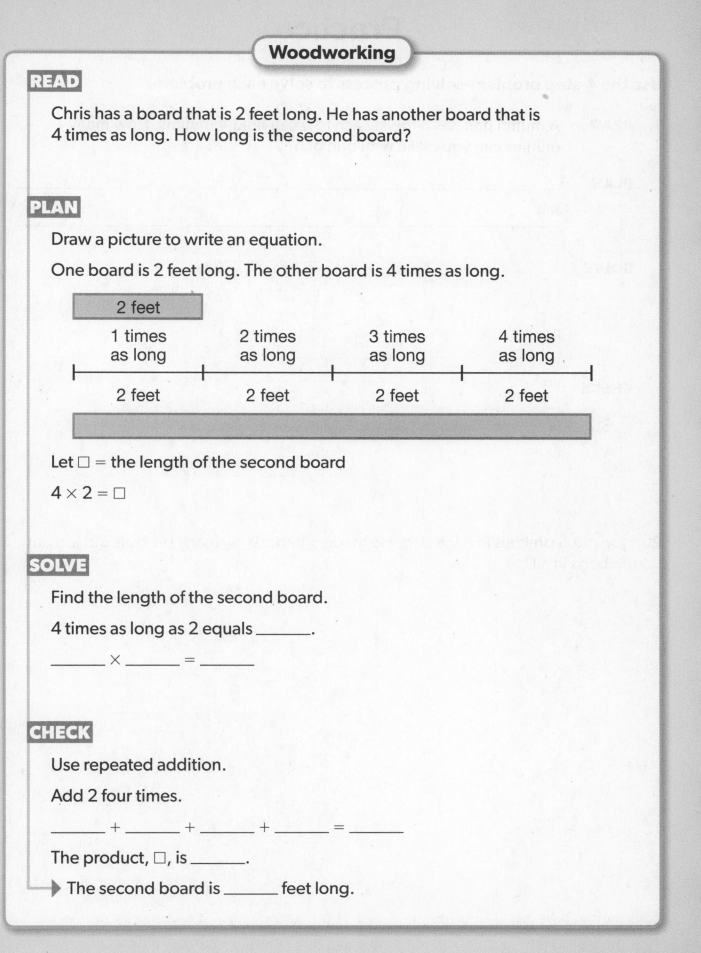

Let □ = the length of the second board

$4 \times 2 = □$

SOLVE

Find the length of the second board.

4 times as long as 2 equals _____.

_____ × _____ = _____

CHECK

Use repeated addition.

Add 2 four times.

_____ + _____ + _____ + _____ = _____

The product, □, is _____.

▶ The second board is _____ feet long.

Practice

Use the 4-step problem-solving process to solve each problem.

1. **READ**   A muffin pan has 3 rows. Each row can hold 4 muffins. How many muffins can you make with one pan?

   PLAN _____

   _____

   SOLVE

   CHECK

2. Joe put 5 pretzels in each bag. He made 5 bags. How many pretzels did Joe put in bags in all?

3. A puppy weighs 4 pounds. A dog weighs 7 times as much as the puppy. How many pounds does the dog weigh?

4. A recipe for punch uses 8 liters of juice. For a school party, Mai needs 8 times as much punch as the recipe makes. How many liters of juice does Mai need?

5. Tammy wants to make 5 bracelets. She needs 9 inches of string for each bracelet. How many inches of string does Tammy need to make the bracelets?

Problem Solving: Division

Stamp Array

READ

George put 24 stamps in 4 equal rows. How many stamps are in each row?

PLAN

Make an array to write an equation.

Draw 24 stamps in 4 equal rows.

Let □ = how many stamps are in each row

$24 \div 4 = \square$

SOLVE

Find the number of stamps in each row.

Divide 24 into 4 equal rows. There are _____ in each row.

_____ ÷ _____ = _____

CHECK

Use **repeated subtraction**.

Subtract 4 from 24 until you reach 0.

$24 - 4 = 20$

$20 - 4 = $ _____

$16 - $ _____ $ = $ _____

_____ − _____ = _____

_____ − _____ = _____

_____ − _____ = _____

You subtracted _____ times.

The quotient, □, is _____.

▶ There are _____ stamps in each row.

Kickball Teams

READ

There are 32 students in gym class for kickball. Ms. Krauss put the students in equal teams of 8 students. How many teams will play kickball?

PLAN

Draw a picture to write an equation.

There are 32 students. 8 students will be on each team.

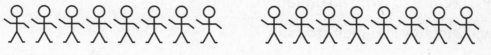

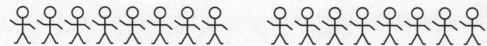

Let □ = the number of kickball teams

32 ÷ 8 = □

SOLVE

Find the number of teams.

32 students divided into teams of 8 make _____ equal teams.

_____ ÷ _____ = _____

CHECK

Use repeated subtraction.

Subtract 8 from 32 until you reach 0.

    32 − _____ = _____

    _____ − _____ = _____

    _____ − _____ = _____

    _____ − _____ = _____

You subtracted _____ times.

The quotient, □, is _____.

▶ There will be _____ teams playing kickball.

Bulletin Board Decorations

READ

Aiden is decorating the bulletin board. He has 42 inches of border paper. He cuts the paper into strips. Each strip is 6 inches long. How many strips can Aiden make?

PLAN

Draw a picture to write an equation.

Show 42 inches in 6-inch strips.

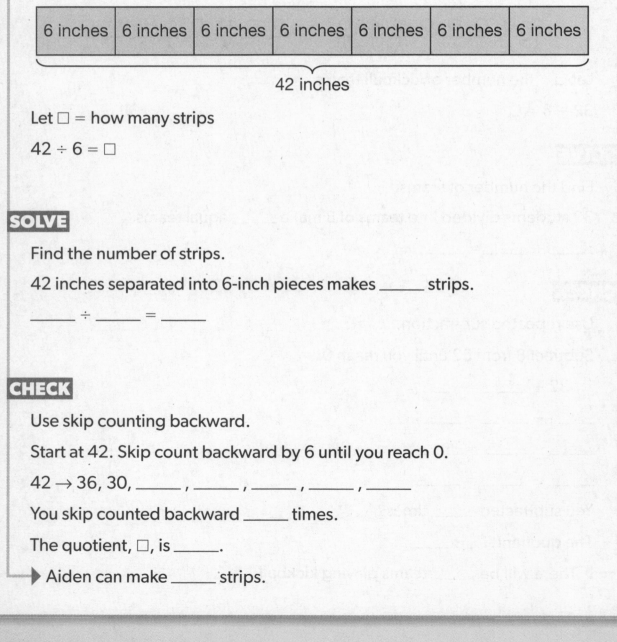

Let □ = how many strips

$42 \div 6 = \square$

SOLVE

Find the number of strips.

42 inches separated into 6-inch pieces makes _____ strips.

_____ ÷ _____ = _____

CHECK

Use skip counting backward.

Start at 42. Skip count backward by 6 until you reach 0.

42 → 36, 30, _____ , _____ , _____ , _____ , _____

You skip counted backward _____ times.

The quotient, □, is _____.

▶ Aiden can make _____ strips.

Fences

READ

A fence is 18 meters long. That is 6 times as long as each section of the fence. How long is each section of the fence?

PLAN

Use a number line to write an equation.

Skip count backward by 6 starting at 18.

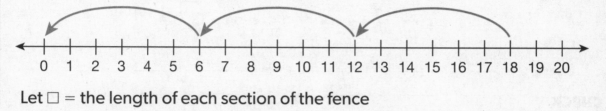

Let □ = the length of each section of the fence

18 ÷ 6 = □

SOLVE

Find how long each section of the fence is.

18 is 6 times as long as _____.

_____ ÷ _____ = _____

CHECK

Use repeated subtraction.

Subtract 6 from 18 until you reach 0.

18 − 6 = _____

_____ − _____ = _____

_____ − _____ = _____

You subtracted _____ times.

The quotient, □, is _____.

▶ Each section of the fence is _____ meters long.

Practice

Use the 4-step problem-solving process to solve each problem.

1. **READ**   Dianna used 28 stars to make a design. She drew 7 stars in each row. How many rows of stars are in Dianna's design?

   PLAN _____

   _____

   SOLVE

   CHECK

2. A poster is 72 inches long. That length is 9 times as long as a picture. How many inches long is the picture?

3. Jake has 30 dimes. He put 5 dimes in each pile. How many piles of dimes did Jake make?

4. Vicki spent 40 minutes making paper cranes. She spent 8 minutes on each crane. How many cranes did Vicki make?

5. A bear weighs 54 pounds. That is 6 times as much as a cub weighs. How many pounds does the cub weigh?

Relating Multiplication and Division

UNDERSTAND Use models to find a missing number in a multiplication equation.

Find the value of △.

$7 \times \triangle = 21$

1 The product is 21.
Take 21 counters.

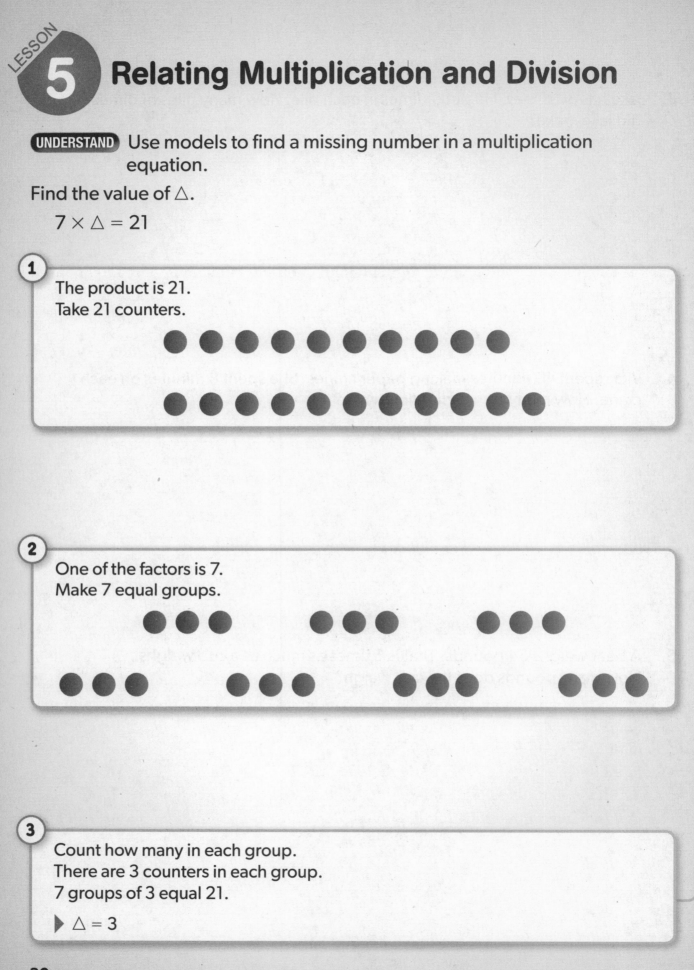

2 One of the factors is 7.
Make 7 equal groups.

3 Count how many in each group.
There are 3 counters in each group.
7 groups of 3 equal 21.

▶ △ = 3

← Connect

Find the value of △.

$$7 \times \triangle = 21$$

1

Read the equation.

7 times a number equals 21.

△ is one of the factors.

2

Use skip counting.

Use a number line to skip count by 7 until you reach 21.

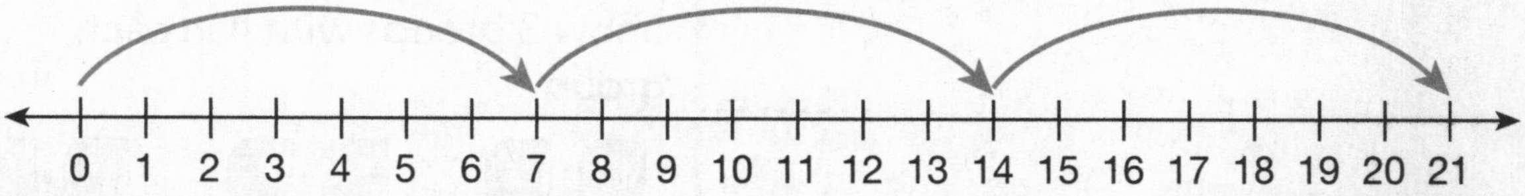

3

Count how many times you skip counted by 7.

You skip counted 3 times.

$$7 \times 3 = 21$$

▶ △ = 3

TRY

Show how to use skip counting to solve for △ in $2 \times \triangle = 8$.

EXAMPLE A Find the value of □.

$$□ ÷ 3 = 4$$

1

Read the equation.

A number divided by 3 equals 4.

□ is the dividend, the total number.

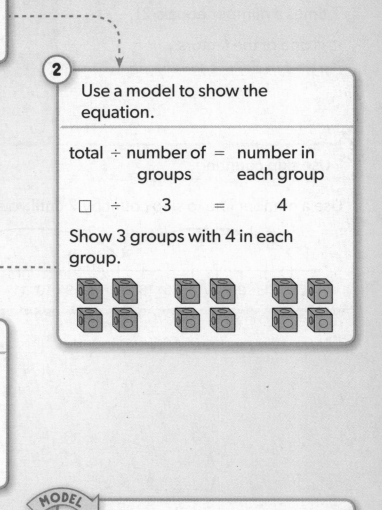

2

Use a model to show the equation.

total ÷ number of = number in
groups   each group

□ ÷ 3 = 4

Show 3 groups with 4 in each group.

3

Find the total.

There are 12 in all.

12 divided by 3 equals 4.

$$12 ÷ 3 = 4$$

▶ □ = 12

MODEL

Draw a model to show how to solve for □ in □ ÷ 6 = 2.

EXAMPLE B Find the value of □.

$$36 \div 4 = \square$$

1

Read the equation.

36 divided by 4 equals a number.

□ is the quotient.

2

Division and multiplication are **inverse operations**.
Write the division equation as a multiplication equation.

Write $36 \div 4 = \square$ as $\square \times 4 = 36$.

3

Find the number that you multiply 4 by to get 36.

$\square \times 4 = 36$

$9 \times 4 = 36$

Since $9 \times 4 = 36$, then $36 \div 4 = 9$.

▶ $\square = 9$

TRY

Use multiplication to find the value of □ in $24 \div 4 = \square$.

EXAMPLE C Use the numbers 5, 7, and 35 to write four equations.

1

Write the **fact family** for the numbers 5, 7, and 35.

Think about multiplication and division facts that use the numbers.

2

Write the multiplication equations.

5	×	7	=	35
factor		factor		product
7	×	5	=	35
factor		factor		product

3

Write the division equations.

35	÷	5	=	7
dividend		divisor		quotient
35	÷	7	=	5
dividend		divisor		quotient

▶ The four equations are:

$5 \times 7 = 35$

$7 \times 5 = 35$

$35 \div 5 = 7$

$35 \div 7 = 5$

DISCUSS

Explain how multiplication and division facts in a fact family are related. Give an example.

FACT FAMILIES

Make a fact family with the numbers in each triangle.
Fill in each box with a number.
Fill in each circle with a symbol (×, ÷, or =).

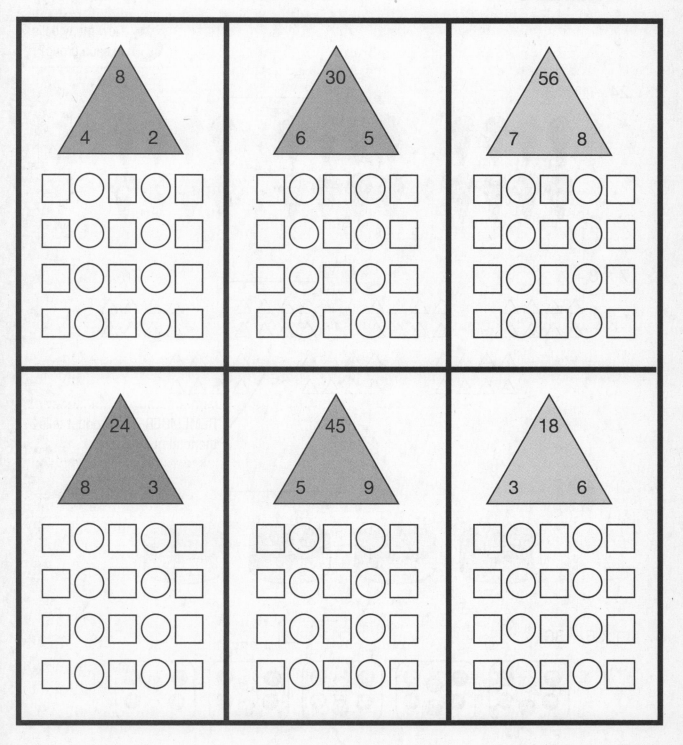

Practice

Write the missing number in each equation.

1. $4 \times \triangle = 20$ $\triangle =$ _____

HINT How many balls in each group?

2. $24 \div \square = 3$ $\square =$ _____

3. $7 \times 8 = \triangle$ $\triangle =$ _____

REMEMBER The product tells the total number.

4. $\square \div 4 = 7$ $\square =$ _____

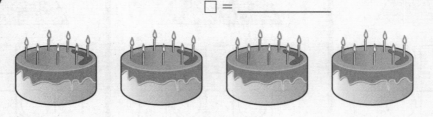

5. $\square \times 6 = 30$ $\square =$ _____

Choose the equation you can use to find the quotient.

6. $63 \div 9 = \square$

   A. $6 \times 9 = 54$

   B. $7 \times 8 = 56$

   C. $7 \times 9 = 63$

   D. $8 \times 9 = 72$

7. $32 \div 8 = \square$

   A. $4 \times 8 = 32$

   B. $8 \times 6 = 48$

   C. $8 \times 7 = 56$

   D. $9 \times 4 = 36$

Use the numbers to write a fact family.

8. 2, 9, 18

_____

_____

_____

_____

9. 3, 7, 21

_____

_____

_____

_____

Solve.

10. A diner has 54 chairs. Each of the 9 tables has the same number of chairs. How many chairs are at each table?

_____

11. Howard bought 6 bags of treats. Each bag has 8 treats. How many treats did Howard buy in all?

_____

12. (SHOW) Draw a picture to show the value of $\triangle$ in $3 \times \triangle = 9$.

13. (WRITE MATH) Explain how you can use a multiplication equation to find $36 \div 6$.

_____

_____

_____

Applying Properties of Operations

UNDERSTAND Use the properties of multiplication to help you learn multiplication facts.

Show that the product of 3 × 4 is the same as the product of 4 × 3.

1

Draw an array for 3 × 4.
Make 3 rows.
Put 4 counters in each row.

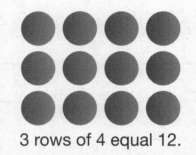

3 rows of 4 equal 12.

2

Draw an array for 4 × 3.
Make 4 rows.
Put 3 counters in each row.

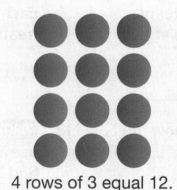

4 rows of 3 equal 12.

3

Both arrays have the same number of counters.
3 × 4 = 12
4 × 3 = 12

▶ The models show that 3 × 4 and 4 × 3 have the same product, 12.

←Connect

Show that the product of 3 × 4 is the same as the product of 4 × 3.

1

Use a multiplication table.
Find the product of 3 × 4.

×	0	1	2	3	4	5
0	0	0	0	0	0	0
1	0	1	2	3	4	5
2	0	2	4	6	8	10
3	0	3	6	9	12	15
4	0	4	8	**12**	16	20
5	0	5	10	15	20	25

The product is 12.

2

Use a multiplication table.
Find the product of 4 × 3.

×	0	1	2	3	4	5
0	0	0	0	0	0	0
1	0	1	2	3	4	5
2	0	2	4	6	8	10
3	0	3	6	9	**12**	15
4	0	4	8	12	16	20
5	0	5	10	15	20	25

The product is also 12.

3

Look at the factors and the products.

The factors are the same, but they are in a different order.

The products are the same.

▶ 3 × 4 and 4 × 3 have the same product, 12.

TRY

What other multiplication fact uses the same numbers as 2 × 3 = 6?

EXAMPLE A Lindsay writes the equation $5 \times 6 = 30$.

Use the **commutative property of multiplication** to write another equation.

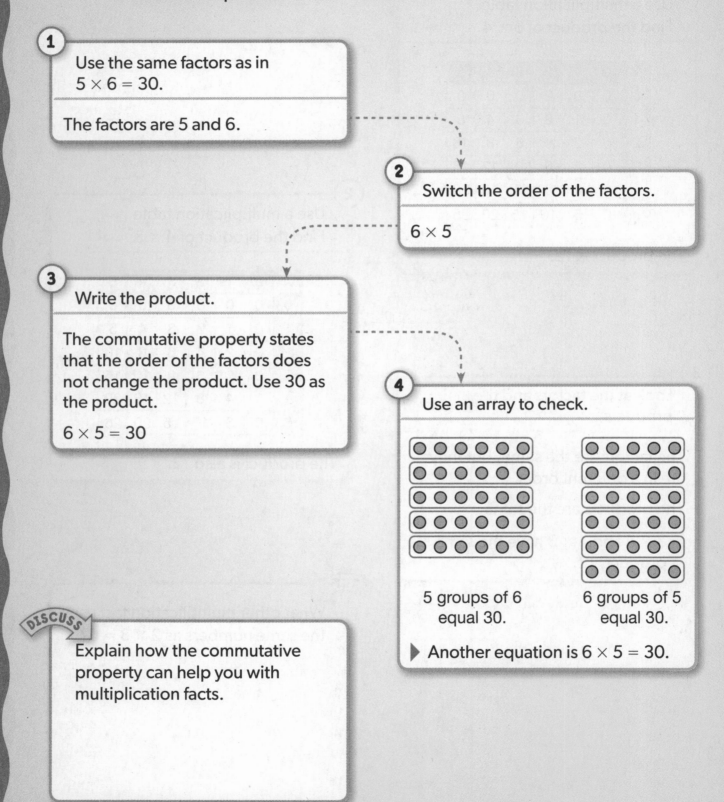

1

Use the same factors as in $5 \times 6 = 30$.

The factors are 5 and 6.

2

Switch the order of the factors.

6×5

3

Write the product.

The commutative property states that the order of the factors does not change the product. Use 30 as the product.

$6 \times 5 = 30$

4

Use an array to check.

5 groups of 6 equal 30.

6 groups of 5 equal 30.

▶ Another equation is $6 \times 5 = 30$.

DISCUSS

Explain how the commutative property can help you with multiplication facts.

EXAMPLE B Use the **associative property of multiplication** to find the product.

$$2 \times 3 \times 4 = \square$$

1

Multiply the first two factors.

$\underbrace{2 \times 3}_{6} \times 4$

$6 \quad \times 4$

2

Multiply by the third factor.

$2 \times 3 \times 4 = 6 \times 4$

$= 24$

3

Use models to check.

Make 2 rows of 3. Make 4 groups.

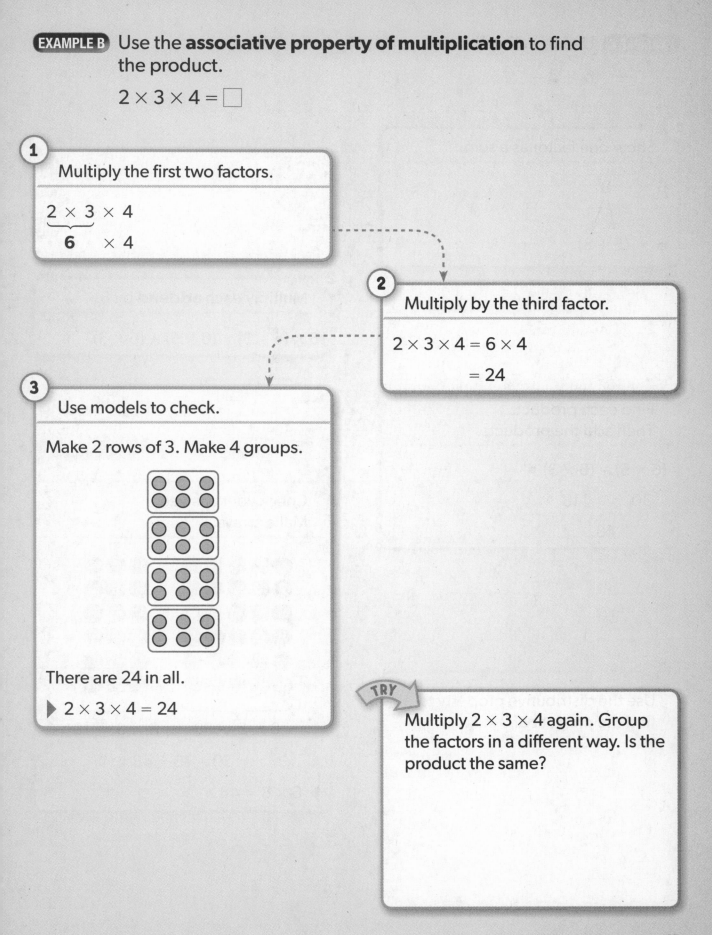

There are 24 in all.

▶ $2 \times 3 \times 4 = 24$

TRY

Multiply $2 \times 3 \times 4$ again. Group the factors in a different way. Is the product the same?

EXAMPLE C Use the **distributive property** to find the product.

$6 \times 8 = \square$

1

Show one factor as a sum.

$6 \times \quad 8$

$6 \times (5 + 3)$

2

Multiply each **addend** by 6.

$6 \times (5 + 3) = (6 \times 5) + (6 \times 3)$

3

Find each product.
Then add the products.

$(6 \times 5) + (6 \times 3)$

$\quad 30 \quad + \quad 18$

$\qquad 48$

4

Check your answer.
Make arrays.

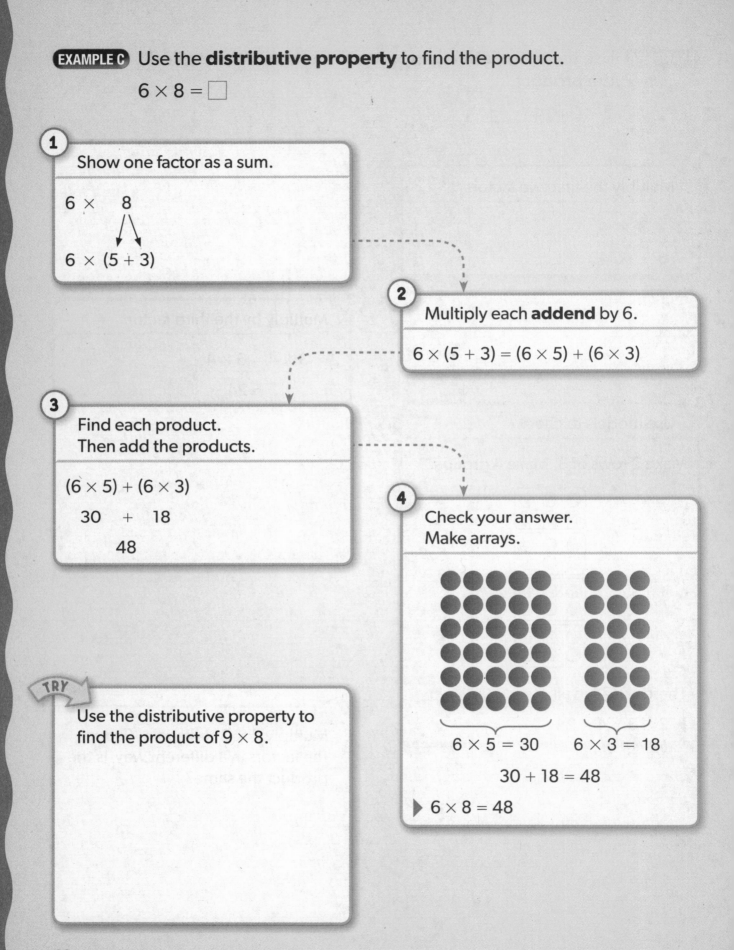

$6 \times 5 = 30 \qquad 6 \times 3 = 18$

$30 + 18 = 48$

▶ $6 \times 8 = 48$

TRY

Use the distributive property to find the product of 9×8.

⚙ Problem Solving

READ

The first baseball cards were printed in the late 1860s. In 1933, a company in Boston was the first to put bubble gum in with baseball cards. The company also printed facts about baseball players on the backs of cards.

Kyle bought 7 packs of baseball cards. Each pack has 6 cards. How many cards did Kyle buy in all?

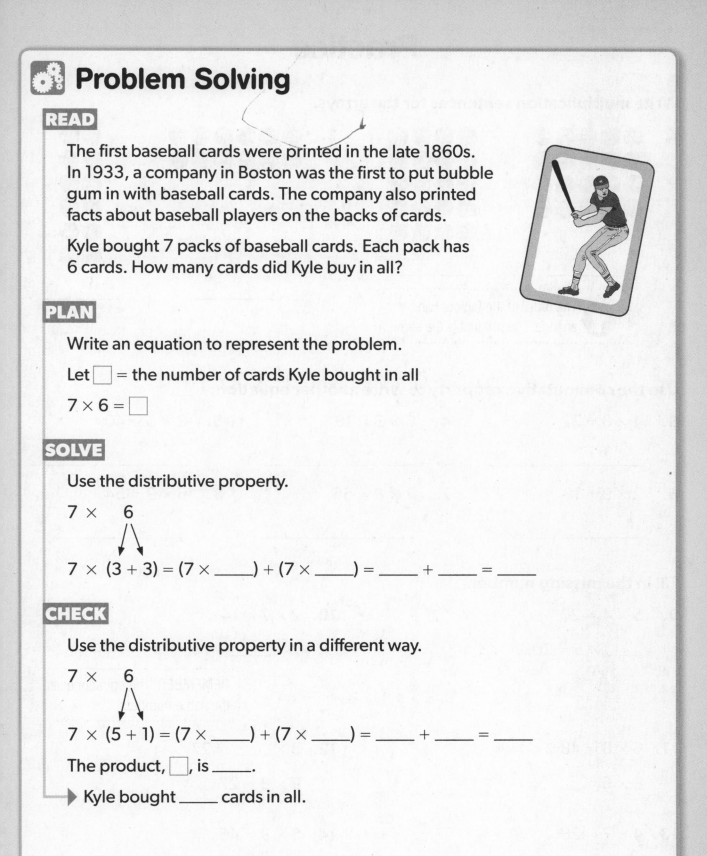

PLAN

Write an equation to represent the problem.

Let ☐ = the number of cards Kyle bought in all

$7 \times 6 = $ ☐

SOLVE

Use the distributive property.

$7 \times \quad 6$

$7 \times (3 + 3) = (7 \times \underline{\quad}) + (7 \times \underline{\quad}) = \underline{\quad} + \underline{\quad} = \underline{\quad}$

CHECK

Use the distributive property in a different way.

$7 \times \quad 6$

$7 \times (5 + 1) = (7 \times \underline{\quad}) + (7 \times \underline{\quad}) = \underline{\quad} + \underline{\quad} = \underline{\quad}$

The product, ☐, is \underline{\quad}.

▶ Kyle bought \underline{\quad} cards in all.

Practice

Write multiplication sentences for the arrays.

1.

_____   _____

2.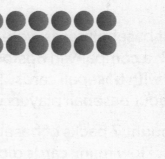

_____   _____

 HINT The order of the factors can change. The product is the same.

Use the commutative property to write another equation.

3. $4 \times 8 = 32$

_____

4. $6 \times 3 = 18$

_____

5. $8 \times 5 = 40$

_____

6. $2 \times 9 = 18$

_____

7. $7 \times 8 = 56$

_____

8. $6 \times 9 = 54$

_____

Fill in the missing number.

9. $5 \times 4 = 20$

____ $\times 5 = 20$

10. $2 \times 7 = 14$

$7 \times$ ____ $= 14$

REMEMBER The equations use the same numbers.

11. $6 \times 8 = 48$

$8 \times 6 =$ ____

12. $3 \times$ ____ $= 27$

$9 \times 3 = 27$

13. $4 \times 7 = 28$

____ $\times 4 = 28$

14. $5 \times 9 = 45$

$9 \times 5 =$ ____

Find the product. Show how you multiply.

15. $3 \times 3 \times 2 =$ _____

16. $5 \times 2 \times 4 =$ _____

17. $6 \times 1 \times 5 =$ _____

18. $2 \times 3 \times 8 =$ _____

Choose the best answer.

19. 4×5

    A. $4 \times (2 \times 3)$

    B. $4 \times (2 + 3)$

    C. $4 + (2 + 3)$

    D. $4 + (2 + 3)$

20. 7×9

    A. $7 + (4 \times 5)$

    B. $7 \times (4 \times 5)$

    C. $7 + (4 + 5)$

    D. $7 \times (4 + 5)$

21. $3 \times (2 + 2)$

    A. $(3 \times 2) \times (3 \times 2)$

    B. $(3 + 2) \times (3 + 2)$

    C. $(3 \times 2) + (3 \times 2)$

    D. $(3 + 2) + (3 + 2)$

22. $5 \times (2 + 5)$

    A. $(5 \times 2) + (5 \times 5)$

    B. $(5 \times 2) \times (5 \times 5)$

    C. $(5 + 2) + (5 + 5)$

    D. $(5 + 2) \times (5 + 5)$

Solve.

23. **DEMONSTRATE** Make a drawing to show that 3×5 and 5×3 have the same product.

24. **CREATE** Write a real world problem with the equation $2 \times 2 \times 3 = 12$.

_____

_____

Multiplying and Dividing Whole Numbers

EXAMPLE A Multiply. $5 \times 6 = \square$

1 Make an array.

Make 5 rows.

Put 6 Xs in each row.

X X X X X X
X X X X X X
X X X X X X
X X X X X X
X X X X X X

2 Count the number of Xs in the array.

There are 30 Xs.

▶ $5 \times 6 = 30$

EXAMPLE B Multiply. $3 \times 9 = \square$

1 Use repeated addition.

Think: 3×9 means 3 groups of 9.

Add 9 three times.

$9 + 9 + 9$

2 Find the sum.

$9 + 9 + 9 = 27$

3 groups of 9 is 27.

▶ $3 \times 9 = 27$

TRY

Multiply. $5 \times 3 = \square$

EXAMPLE C Find the product. $8 \times 7 = \square$

1

Use the distributive property.

Show one factor as a sum.

$8 \times 7 = 8 \times (5 + 2)$

2

Multiply each addend by 8.
Add the products.

$(8 \times 5) + (8 \times 2)$

40 + 16

56

▶ $8 \times 7 = 56$

EXAMPLE D Find the product. $4 \times 6 = \square$

1

Use skip counting.

4×6 means 4 groups of 6.

Skip count by 6. Skip count four times.

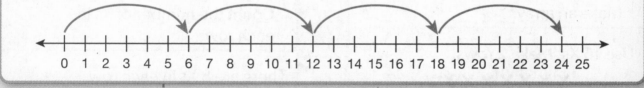

0 1 2 3 4 5 6 7 8 9 10 11 12 13 14 15 16 17 18 19 20 21 22 23 24 25

2

Find the product.

The product is the number where the last arrow lands.

▶ $4 \times 6 = 24$

DISCUSS

Describe which strategy you would use to multiply $8 \times 8 = \square$.

EXAMPLE E Divide. $35 \div 5 = \square$

1

Use repeated subtraction.

Subtract 5 from 35 until you reach 0.

$35 - 5 = 30$

$30 - 5 = 25$

$25 - 5 = 20$

$20 - 5 = 15$

$15 - 5 = 10$

$10 - 5 = 5$

$5 - 5 = 0$

2

Count how many times you subtracted.

You subtracted 5 from 35 a total of 7 times.

The quotient is 7.

▶ $35 \div 5 = 7$

EXAMPLE F Divide. $16 \div 2 = \square$

1

Make an array.

Use 16 Xs. Make 2 rows.

X X X X X X X X
X X X X X X X X

2

Count the number of Xs in each row.

There are 8 Xs in each row.

▶ $16 \div 2 = 8$

TRY

Divide. $18 \div 3 = \square$

EXAMPLE G Divide. $32 \div 4 = \square$

1

Write the division equation as a multiplication equation.

Write $32 \div 4 = \square$ as $\square \times 4 = 32$.

2

Think of a multiplication fact that uses the same numbers.

What number do you multiply 4 by to get 32?

$\square \times 4 = 32$

$\mathbf{8} \times 4 = 32$

Since $8 \times 4 = 32$, then $32 \div 4 = 8$.

▶ $32 \div 4 = 8$

EXAMPLE H Divide. $36 \div 9 = \square$

1

Write the division equation as a multiplication equation.

Write $36 \div 9 = \square$ as $\square \times 9 = 36$.

2

Think of a multiplication fact that uses the same numbers.

Find the number that you multiply 9 by to get 36.

$\square \times 9 = 36$

$\mathbf{4} \times 9 = 36$

Since $4 \times 9 = 36$, then $36 \div 9 = 4$.

▶ $36 \div 9 = 4$

DISCUSS

Explain why you are able to use a multiplication fact to solve a division equation.

Practice

Skip count to find the product.

1. $5 \times 8 = $ _____

_____, _____, _____, _____, _____

> **HINT** How many times do you skip count by 8?

2. $4 \times 7 = $ _____

_____, _____, _____, _____

Use repeated addition to find the product.

3. $6 \times 4 = $ _____

_____ + _____ + _____ + _____ + _____ + _____ = _____

4. $5 \times 9 = $ _____

_____ + _____ + _____ + _____ + _____ = _____

Find the products.

5. $6 \times 3 = $ _____

$3 \times 6 = $ _____

6. $9 \times 2 = $ _____

$2 \times 9 = $ _____

7. $8 \times 4 = $ _____

$4 \times 8 = $ _____

8. $5 \times 7 = $ _____

$7 \times 5 = $ _____

9. $9 \times 4 = $ _____

$4 \times 9 = $ _____

10. $9 \times 8 = $ _____

$8 \times 9 = $ _____

> **REMEMBER** The order of the factors does not change the product.

Use repeated subtraction to find the quotient.

11. $24 \div 6 = $ _____

$24 - $ _____ $= $ _____

_____ $- $ _____ $= $ _____

_____ $- $ _____ $= $ _____

_____ $- $ _____ $= $ _____

12. $45 \div 9 = $ _____

$45 - $ _____ $= $ _____

_____ $- $ _____ $= $ _____

_____ $- $ _____ $= $ _____

_____ $- $ _____ $= $ _____

_____ $- $ _____ $= $ _____

Write a multiplication fact you can use to find the quotient.

13. $28 \div 4 =$ _____

_____

14. $18 \div 2 =$ _____

_____

15. $35 \div 5 =$ _____

_____

16. $42 \div 7 =$ _____

_____

17. $15 \div 5 =$ _____

_____

18. $16 \div 8 =$ _____

_____

Write the product or quotient.

19. $4 \times 3 =$ _____

20. $5 \times 2 =$ _____

21. $7 \times 3 =$ _____

22. $9 \times 4 =$ _____

23. $6 \times 3 =$ _____

24. $3 \times 8 =$ _____

25. $5 \times 7 =$ _____

26. $8 \times 1 =$ _____

27. $12 \div 6 =$ _____

28. $40 \div 5 =$ _____

29. $28 \div 7 =$ _____

30. $36 \div 9 =$ _____

31. $18 \div 3 =$ _____

32. $24 \div 4 =$ _____

33. $32 \div 8 =$ _____

34. $7 \div 1 =$ _____

35. $10 \div 5 =$ _____

36. $56 \div 7 =$ _____

37. $9 \times 5 =$ _____

38. $14 \div 2 =$ _____

39. $2 \times 3 =$ _____

40. $35 \div 5 =$ _____

41. $4 \times 4 =$ _____

42. $9 \div 9 =$ _____

43. $5 \times 4 =$ _____

44. $15 \div 3 =$ _____

45. $5 \times 6 =$ _____

Solve.

46. (DRAW) Draw an array that could be used to find the quotient of $24 \div 3$.

47. (WRITE) Explain how you would use the distributive property to find the product of 5×9.

_____

_____

Problem Solving: Two-Step Word Problems

Stamp Collecting

READ

Hank has 115 stamps. Michael has 95 more stamps than Hank. Pedro has 28 fewer stamps than Michael. How many stamps does Pedro have?

PLAN

Step 1: Write an equation to find the number of stamps Michael has.

Let m = the number of stamps Michael has

$115 + 95 = m$

Step 2: Use the answer from Step 1. Write an equation to find the number of stamps Pedro has.

Let p = the number of stamps Pedro has

number of stamps Michael has − 28 = p

SOLVE

Step 1: Add.

115 ← addend
$+ \ 95$ ← addend
_____ ← **sum**

Step 2: Subtract.

210 ← **minuend**
$- \ 28$ ← **subtrahend**
_____ ← **difference**

CHECK

You can estimate to decide if your answer is reasonable.

Step 1: Round the addends.

$100 + 100 =$ _____

Step 2: Round the minuend and subtrahend.

$200 - 30 = 170$ ← 182 is close to 170. The answer is reasonable.

The difference, p, is _____.

▶ Pedro has _____ stamps.

Art Box

READ

In Jenny's art box, there are 4 green markers. There are three times as many blue markers as green markers. How many green and blue markers are in Jenny's art box in all?

PLAN

Step 1: Write an equation to find the number of blue markers Jenny has.

Let p = the number of blue markers

$3 \times 4 = p$

Step 2: Use the answer from Step 1. Write an equation to find the number of green and blue markers Jenny has in all.

Let m = the number of green and blue markers in all

number of blue markers + 4 = m

SOLVE

Step 1: Multiply.

$$
\begin{array}{r}
4 \leftarrow \text{factor} \\
\times\ 3 \leftarrow \text{factor} \\
\hline
 \leftarrow \text{product}
\end{array}
$$

Step 2: Add.

$$
\begin{array}{r}
12 \leftarrow \text{addend} \\
+\ 4 \leftarrow \text{addend} \\
\hline
 \leftarrow \text{sum}
\end{array}
$$

CHECK

Draw a picture to see if your answer makes sense.

There are _____ markers in all.

Does your answer make sense? _____

▶ Altogether, there are _____ green and blue markers in Jenny's art box.

Camera Shopping

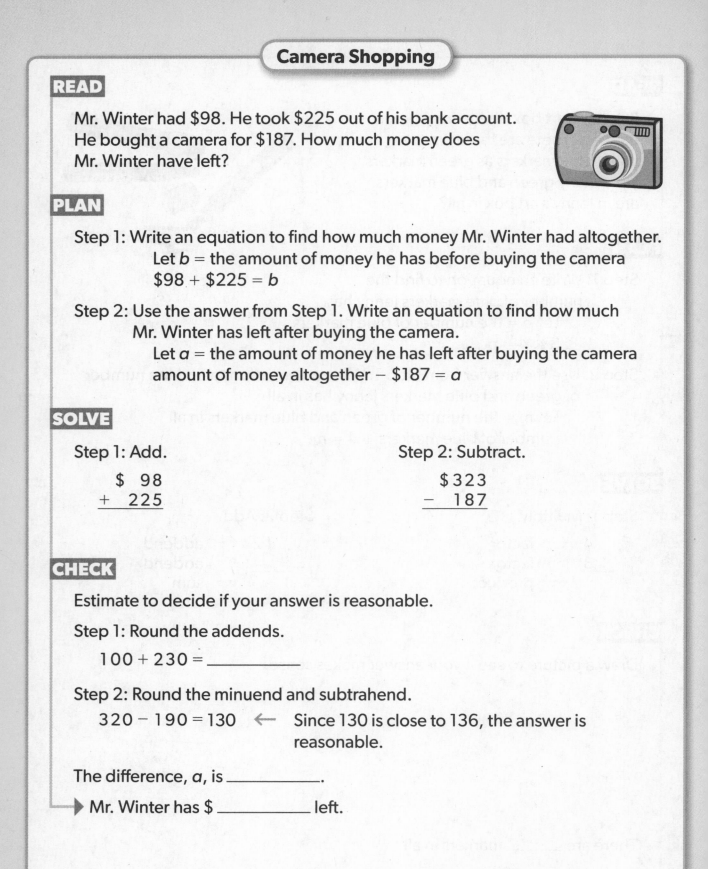

READ

Mr. Winter had $98. He took $225 out of his bank account. He bought a camera for $187. How much money does Mr. Winter have left?

PLAN

Step 1: Write an equation to find how much money Mr. Winter had altogether.
Let b = the amount of money he has before buying the camera
$98 + $225 = b$

Step 2: Use the answer from Step 1. Write an equation to find how much Mr. Winter has left after buying the camera.
Let a = the amount of money he has left after buying the camera
amount of money altogether − $187 = a$

SOLVE

Step 1: Add.

$$\begin{array}{r} \$\ \ 98 \\ +\ \ 225 \\ \hline \end{array}$$

Step 2: Subtract.

$$\begin{array}{r} \$323 \\ -\ \ 187 \\ \hline \end{array}$$

CHECK

Estimate to decide if your answer is reasonable.

Step 1: Round the addends.

$100 + 230 = $ _____

Step 2: Round the minuend and subtrahend.

$320 - 190 = 130$ ← Since 130 is close to 136, the answer is reasonable.

The difference, a, is _____.

▶ Mr. Winter has $ _____ left.

Gift Bags

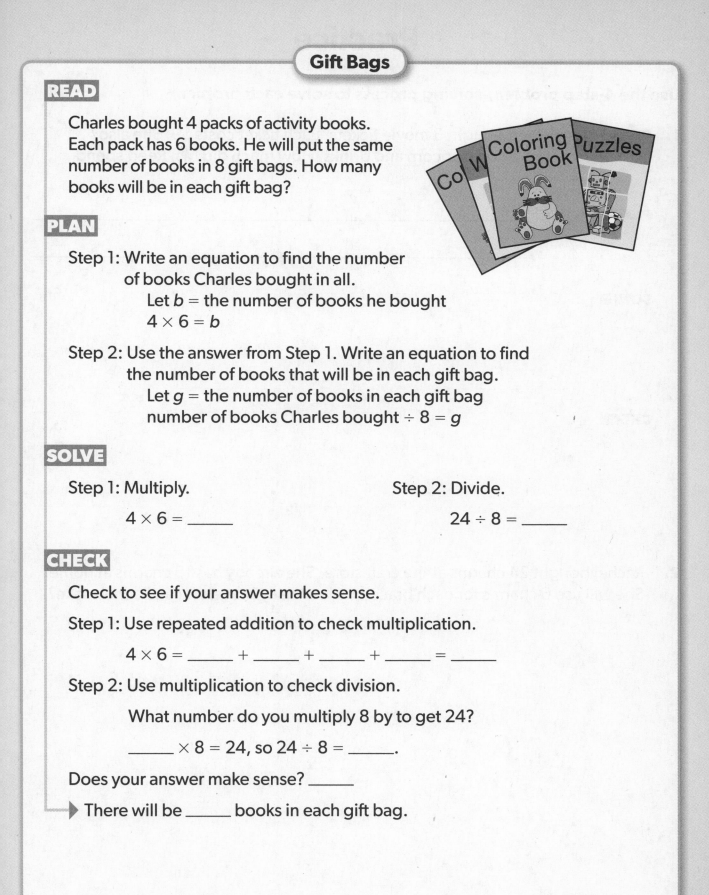

READ

Charles bought 4 packs of activity books. Each pack has 6 books. He will put the same number of books in 8 gift bags. How many books will be in each gift bag?

PLAN

Step 1: Write an equation to find the number of books Charles bought in all.

Let b = the number of books he bought

$4 \times 6 = b$

Step 2: Use the answer from Step 1. Write an equation to find the number of books that will be in each gift bag.

Let g = the number of books in each gift bag

number of books Charles bought $\div$ 8 = g

SOLVE

Step 1: Multiply.

$4 \times 6 =$ _____

Step 2: Divide.

$24 \div 8 =$ _____

CHECK

Check to see if your answer makes sense.

Step 1: Use repeated addition to check multiplication.

$4 \times 6 =$ _____ + _____ + _____ + _____ = _____

Step 2: Use multiplication to check division.

What number do you multiply 8 by to get 24?

_____ $\times$ 8 = 24, so 24 $\div$ 8 = _____.

Does your answer make sense? _____

▶ There will be _____ books in each gift bag.

Practice

Use the 4-step problem-solving process to solve each problem.

1. **READ**   Ms. Reed bought 3 movie tickets. Each ticket costs $9. She also spent $22 on popcorn and drinks. How much did Ms. Reed spend in all?

   PLAN _____

   _____

   SOLVE

   CHECK

2. Rachel bought 24 charms at the craft store. She already has 18 charms at home. She will use 6 charms for each bracelet. How many bracelets can Rachel make?

3. A book has 288 pages. Owen read 108 pages in the first week. He read 94 pages in the second week. How many more pages does Owen have left to read?

4. There were 9 pizzas at the luncheon. Each pizza had 8 slices. A total of 66 slices were eaten. How many slices of pizza were left?

5. George bought 36 balloons. His plan is to decorate 6 tables with an equal number of balloons. Each balloon costs $2. How much will it cost to decorate each table with balloons?

9 Identifying Patterns

UNDERSTAND A group of numbers can form a **number pattern**.

Find the next number in this pattern.

8, 12, 16, 20, 24, _____?_____

1

Make a drawing to show the pattern.

| 8 | 12 | 16 | 20 | 24 |

2

Find how many more dots there are from one set to the next set in the pattern. Each set of dots has 4 more than the set before it.

3

Find the number of dots in the next set.
The next set has 4 more dots than 24.

| 8 | 12 | 16 | 20 | 24 | 28 |

▶ The next number in the pattern is 28.

⊏ Connect

Find the next number in this pattern.

8, 12, 16, 20, 24, ___?___

1

Use a hundreds chart.

Find the numbers in the pattern.

1	2	3	4	5	6	7	**8**	9	10
11	**12**	13	14	15	**16**	17	18	19	**20**
21	22	23	**24**	25	26	27	28	29	30
31	32	33	34	35	36	37	38	39	40
41	42	43	44	45	46	47	48	49	50
51	52	53	54	55	56	57	58	59	60
61	62	63	64	65	66	67	68	69	70
71	72	73	74	75	76	77	78	79	80
81	82	83	84	85	86	87	88	89	90
91	92	93	94	95	96	97	98	99	100

2

Count from one number in the pattern to the next number.

12 is 4 more than 8.

16 is 4 more than 12.

20 is 4 more than 16.

24 is 4 more than 20.

3

Find the next number in the pattern.

The next number is 4 more than 24.

24 + 4 = 28

▶ The next number in the pattern is 28.

TRY

Find the next two numbers in the pattern after 28.

EXAMPLE A Find the missing number in this pattern.

6, 12, 18, ____?____, 30, 36

1

Use a hundreds chart.

Find the numbers in the pattern.

1	2	3	4	5	**6**	7	8	9	10
11	**12**	13	14	15	16	17	**18**	19	20
21	22	23	24	25	26	27	28	29	**30**
31	32	33	34	35	**36**	37	38	39	40
41	42	43	44	45	46	47	48	49	50
51	52	53	54	55	56	57	58	59	60
61	62	63	64	65	66	67	68	69	70
71	72	73	74	75	76	77	78	79	80
81	82	83	84	85	86	87	88	89	90
91	92	93	94	95	96	97	98	99	100

2

Count from one number to the next number in the pattern.

12 is 6 more than 6.

18 is 6 more than 12.

36 is 6 more than 30.

3

Find the missing number in the pattern.

The number after 18 is 6 more than 18.

$18 + 6 = 24$

▶ The missing number in the pattern is 24.

CHECK

Check that 24 is the correct answer.

Find 6 more than 24. Is it the next number in the pattern?

$24 + 6 = $ _____

EXAMPLE B Find the next number in this pattern.

47, 44, 41, 38, 35, ___?___

1

Look at the numbers in the pattern.

The numbers are decreasing.

This could be a subtraction pattern.

2

Subtract to go from one number to the next number in the pattern.

47 − 44 = 3

44 − 41 = 3

41 − 38 = 3

38 − 35 = 3

Each number is 3 less than the number before it.

3

Find the next number in the pattern.

The next number is 3 less than 35.

35 − 3 = 32

▶ The next number in the pattern is 32.

TRY

Find the next two numbers in the pattern after 32.

EXAMPLE C If you add an **even number** and an **odd number**, is the sum even or odd?

1

Use an addition table.

Add an even number and an odd number.

Try 4 + 9.

+	0	1	2	3	4	5	6	7	8	9	10
0	0	1	2	3	4	5	6	7	8	9	10
1	1	2	3	4	5	6	7	8	9	10	11
2	2	3	4	5	6	7	8	9	10	11	12
3	3	4	5	6	7	8	9	10	11	12	13
4	4	5	6	7	8	9	10	11	12	13	14
5	5	6	7	8	9	10	11	12	13	14	15
6	6	7	8	9	10	11	12	13	14	15	16
7	7	8	9	10	11	12	13	14	15	16	17
8	8	9	10	11	12	13	14	15	16	17	18
9	9	10	11	12	13	14	15	16	17	18	19
10	10	11	12	13	14	15	16	17	18	19	20

4 + 9 = 13

2

Decide if 13 is even or odd.

13 has a 3 in the ones place.

13 is an odd number.

DISCUSS

If you add two even numbers, is the sum even or odd? Give examples.

3

Try other addition problems with an even and an odd addend.

0 + 1 = 1

2 + 3 = 5

6 + 5 = 11

8 + 7 = 15

▶ The sum of an even number and an odd number is always an odd number.

EXAMPLE D If you multiply an even number and an odd number, is the product even or odd?

1

Use a multiplication table.

Multiply an even number and an odd number.

Try 6×5.

×	0	1	2	3	4	5	6	7	8	9	10
0	0	0	0	0	0	0	0	0	0	0	0
1	0	1	2	3	4	5	6	7	8	9	10
2	0	2	4	6	8	10	12	14	16	18	20
3	0	3	6	9	12	15	18	21	24	27	30
4	0	4	8	12	16	20	24	28	32	36	40
5	0	5	10	15	20	25	**30**	35	40	45	50
6	0	6	12	18	24	30	36	42	48	54	60
7	0	7	14	21	28	35	42	49	56	63	70
8	0	8	16	24	32	40	48	56	64	72	80
9	0	9	18	27	36	45	54	63	72	81	90
10	0	10	20	30	40	50	60	70	80	90	100

$6 \times 5 = 30$

2

Decide if 30 is even or odd.

30 has a 0 in the ones place.

30 is an even number.

DISCUSS

If you multiply two odd numbers, is the product even or odd? Give examples.

3

Try other multiplication problems with an even and an odd factor.

$0 \times 1 = 0$

$2 \times 3 = 6$

$4 \times 7 = 28$

$8 \times 9 = 72$

▶ The product of an even number and an odd number is always an even number.

Practice

Draw the dots in the next set in this pattern.

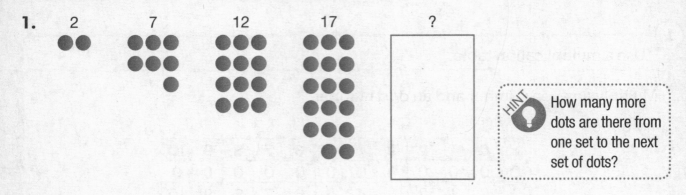

1. 2   7   12   17   ?

HINT How many more dots are there from one set to the next set of dots?

Describe the number pattern.

2. 5, 11, 17, 23, 29

_____

3. 26, 21, 16, 11, 6

_____

4. 7, 14, 21, 28, 35

_____

Find the next number in the pattern.

5. 16, 19, 22, 25, ___?___

6. 31, 36, 41, 46, ___?___

7. 48, 41, 34, 27, ___?___

8. 8, 12, 16, 20, ___?___

Is the sum an odd or even number? Write *odd* or *even*.

9. 0 + 5

10. 8 + 3

11. 4 + 12

Is the product an odd or even number? Write _odd_ or _even_.

12. 2×7

13. 5×3

14. 8×7

_____

_____

_____

Choose the best answer.

15. Chung added a number to 4. The sum was even. Which could be the other number that Chung added?

    A. 3

    B. 5

    C. 6

    D. 7

16. Kayla multiplied a number by 3. The product was odd. Which could be the other number that Kayla multiplied?

    A. 2

    B. 4

    C. 6

    D. 7

Solve.

17. Caroline read 8 pages on Monday, 16 pages on Tuesday, 24 pages on Wednesday, and 32 pages on Thursday. If the pattern continues, how many pages will Caroline read on Friday?

_____

18. APPLY If you multiply an even number by any number, the product is an even number. Give three examples to show that this is true.

_____

19. EXPLAIN How does the distributive property help you know that the product of 8×5 is an even number?

$8 \times 5 = (4 \times 5) + (4 \times \underline{\hspace{1cm}})$

$= \underline{\hspace{1cm}} + \underline{\hspace{1cm}}$

$= \underline{\hspace{1cm}}$

_____

1 Review

Write a multiplication or division sentence.

1. How many tiles in all?

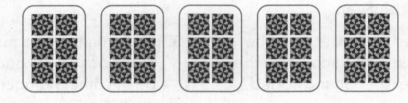

_____ × _____ = _____   _____ tiles

2. How many puppets in each group?

24 ÷ _____ = _____   _____ puppets in each group

Use the picture to write an equation. Then solve the problem.

3. Diego drew 4 rows of ladybugs. He drew 5 ladybugs in each row. How many ladybugs did Diego draw in all?

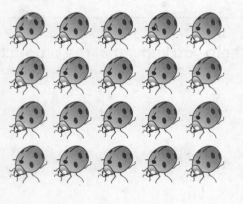

Equation: _____

Diego drew _____ ladybugs.

4. There are 15 rabbits. There are 5 rabbits in each group. How many groups are there?

Equation: _____

There are _____ groups of rabbits.

Multiply or divide.

5. $5 \times 3 = $ _____

6. $9 \times 2 = $ _____

7. $6 \times 5 = $ _____

8. $28 \div 4 = $ _____

9. $56 \div 8 = $ _____

10. $36 \div 9 = $ _____

Write the missing number in each equation.

11. $8 \times \square = 32$

$\square = $ _____

12. $12 \div \triangle = 2$

$\triangle = $ _____

13. $\bigcirc \times 4 = 20$

$\bigcirc = $ _____

Choose the equation you can use to find the quotient.

14. $24 \div 6 = \square$

   A. $6 + 18 = 24$
   B. $6 \times 4 = 24$
   C. $8 \times 3 = 24$
   D. $12 \times 2 = 24$

15. $40 \div 5 = \square$

   A. $8 \times 4 = 32$
   B. $20 + 20 = 40$
   C. $5 \times 8 = 40$
   D. $6 \times 7 = 42$

Use the commutative property to write another equation.

16. $2 \times 4 = 8$ _____

17. $5 \times 9 = 45$ _____

Find the product.

18. $2 \times 4 \times 6 = $ _____

19. $3 \times 2 \times 5 = $ _____

20. $3 \times 5 = 3 \times (2 + 3)$

$= (3 \times \text{\_\_\_\_}) + (3 \times \text{\_\_\_\_})$

$= \text{\_\_\_\_} + \text{\_\_\_\_}$

$= \text{\_\_\_\_}$

21. $7 \times 4 = 7 \times (2 + 2)$

$= (7 \times \text{\_\_\_\_}) + (7 \times \text{\_\_\_\_})$

$= \text{\_\_\_\_} + \text{\_\_\_\_}$

$= \text{\_\_\_\_}$

Find the next number in the pattern.

22. 37, 34, 31, 28, ___?___

_____

23. 6, 12, 18, 24, ___?___

_____

Is the answer an odd or even number? Write *odd* or *even*.

24. $6 + 4$

_____

25. $5 + 8$

_____

26. $7 + 11$

_____

27. 4×6

_____

28. 3×7

_____

29. 6×5

_____

Solve.

30. Joel put 9 carrot sticks in each bag. He made 6 bags of carrot sticks. How many carrot sticks did Joel put in bags?

_____

31. Jane's necklace is 8 inches long. Danielle's necklace is 3 times as long as Jane's necklace. How many inches long is Danielle's necklace?

_____

32. There are 48 students on the playground for field day. Ms. Baldwin will put the students in 8 equal groups. How many students will be in each group?

_____

33. There are 375 people in the auditorium for the talent show. There are 226 students and 30 teachers in the audience. The rest of the people are performers. How many people are performers? Use estimation to check your answer.

_____

34. **DEMONSTRATE** Rebecca planted 8 rows of tomato plants. Each row has 5 plants. How many tomato plants did Rebecca plant? Make an array to show the plants. Then write an equation to solve.

_____

35. **APPLY** At the game store, Mr. Ramos bought 5 games. Each game cost $7. He also spent $25 on batteries. How much did Mr. Ramos spend at the game store? Write equations to show the problem. Then solve the equations.

_____

_____

A TRIP TO THE MUSEUM

There are 32 children going to the museum. The table shows the number of children each type of vehicle can take to the museum.

Type of Vehicle	Minivan	Sport Utility Vehicle (SUV)	Sedan
Number of Students	9 students	6 students	4 students

1. Suppose the parents only have sedans. How many sedans do the parents need to take all the children to the museum? Show your work.

    _____ sedans

2. One parent has a minivan and 3 parents each have a SUV. Will that be enough to take all the children to the museum? Show your work and explain your answer.

    _____

    _____

3. What is the least number of each type of vehicle needed to take all the children? There should be at least one vehicle of each type. Show your work.

    _____ van(s)   _____ SUV(s)   _____ sedan(s)

Grade 2 OA

Represent and solve problems involving addition and subtraction.

Add and subtract within 20.

Work with equal groups of objects to gain foundations for multiplication.

Grade 4 OA

Use the four operations with whole numbers to solve problems.

Gain familiarity with factors and multiples.

Grade 3 NBT

Use place value understanding and properties of operations to perform multi-digit arithmetic.

Grade 2 NBT

Understand place value.

Use place value understanding and properties of operations to add and subtract.

Grade 4 NBT

Generalize place value understanding for multi-digit whole numbers.

Use place value understanding and properties of operations to perform multi-digit arithmetic.

Domain 2
Number and Operations in Base Ten

Using Place Value to Round Whole Numbers

UNDERSTAND You can **round** a number to the nearest ten and to the nearest hundred.

Round 22 to the nearest ten.

1

Show 22 counters.

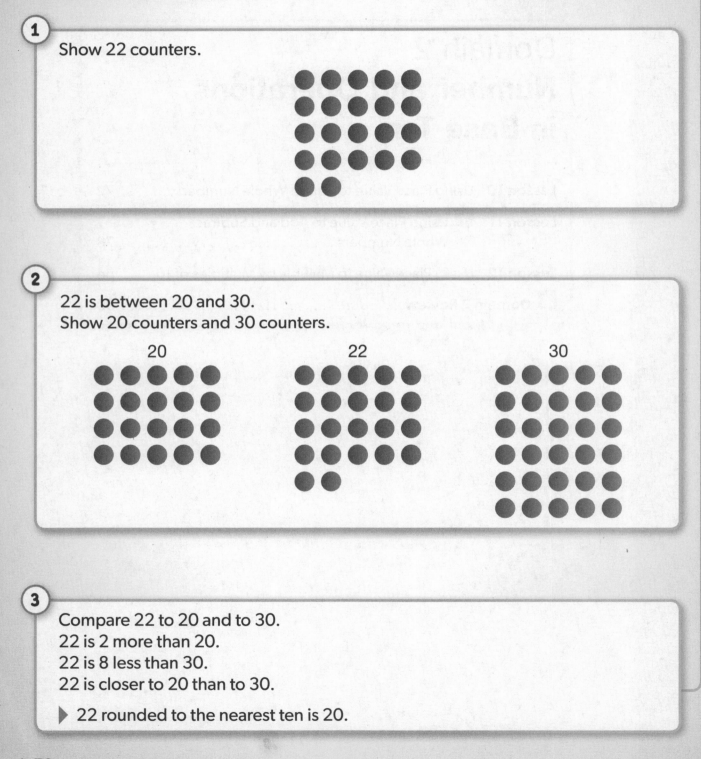

2

22 is between 20 and 30.
Show 20 counters and 30 counters.

20   22   30

3

Compare 22 to 20 and to 30.
22 is 2 more than 20.
22 is 8 less than 30.
22 is closer to 20 than to 30.

▶ 22 rounded to the nearest ten is 20.

⇇ Connect

Round 22 to the nearest ten.

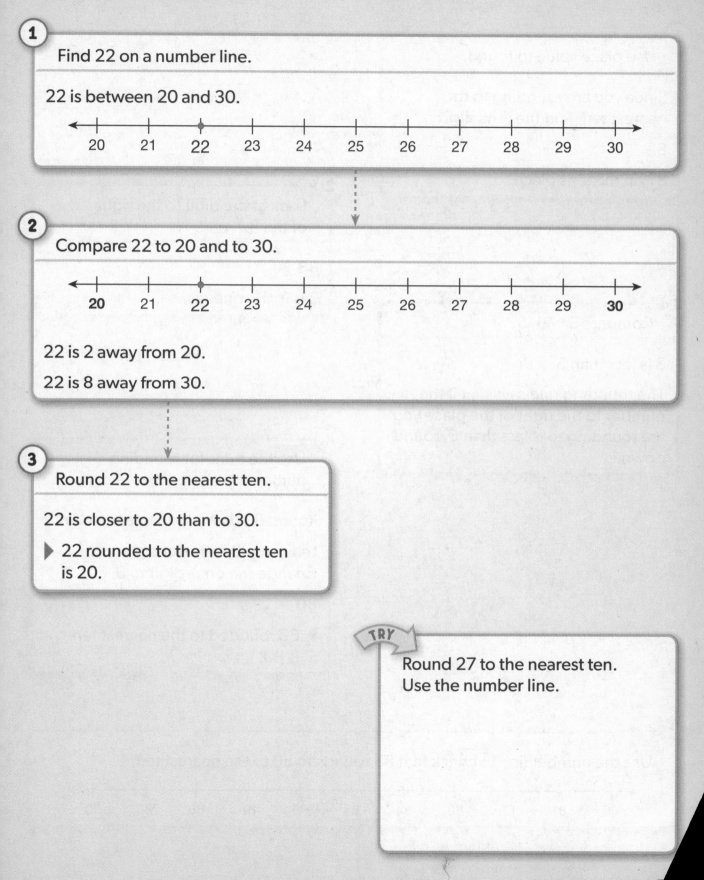

1

Find 22 on a number line.

22 is between 20 and 30.

2

Compare 22 to 20 and to 30.

22 is 2 away from 20.

22 is 8 away from 30.

3

Round 22 to the nearest ten.

22 is closer to 20 than to 30.

▶ 22 rounded to the nearest ten is 20.

TRY

Round 27 to the nearest ten. Use the number line.

EXAMPLE A Round 83 to the nearest ten.

1

Use place value to round.

Since you are rounding to the nearest ten, find the tens **digit**.

<u>8</u>3

8 is in the tens place.

2

Look at the digit to the right of the 8.

8<u>3</u>

3 is in the ones place.

3

Compare 3 with 5.

3 is less than 5.

The rounding rule says that if the number to the right of the place you are rounding to is less than 5, round down.

4

Use the rules for rounding numbers.

Round 83 down to the nearest ten.

Leave the 8 in the tens place. Change the ones digit to 0.

<u>8</u>**0**

▶ 83 rounded to the nearest ten is 80.

CHECK

Use the number line to check that 83 rounds to 80 to the nearest ten.

80 81 82 83 84 85 86 87 88 89 90

Number and Operations in Base Ten

EXAMPLE B Round 284 to the nearest hundred.

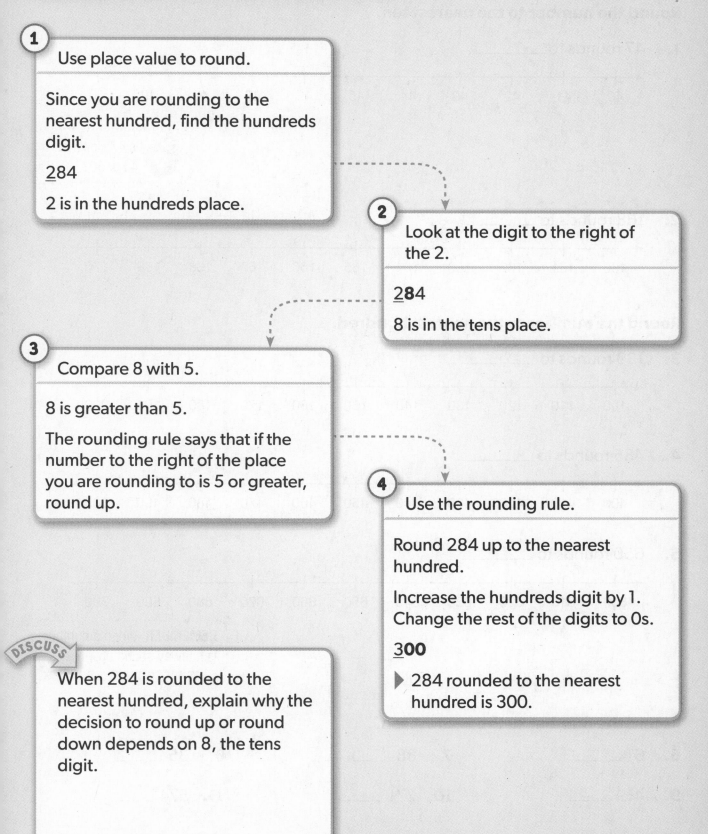

1

Use place value to round.

Since you are rounding to the nearest hundred, find the hundreds digit.

2̲84

2 is in the hundreds place.

2

Look at the digit to the right of the 2.

2̲84

8 is in the tens place.

3

Compare 8 with 5.

8 is greater than 5.

The rounding rule says that if the number to the right of the place you are rounding to is 5 or greater, round up.

4

Use the rounding rule.

Round 284 up to the nearest hundred.

Increase the hundreds digit by 1. Change the rest of the digits to 0s.

3̲00

▶ 284 rounded to the nearest hundred is 300.

DISCUSS

When 284 is rounded to the nearest hundred, explain why the decision to round up or round down depends on 8, the tens digit.

Practice

Round the number to the nearest ten.

1. 47 rounds to _____.

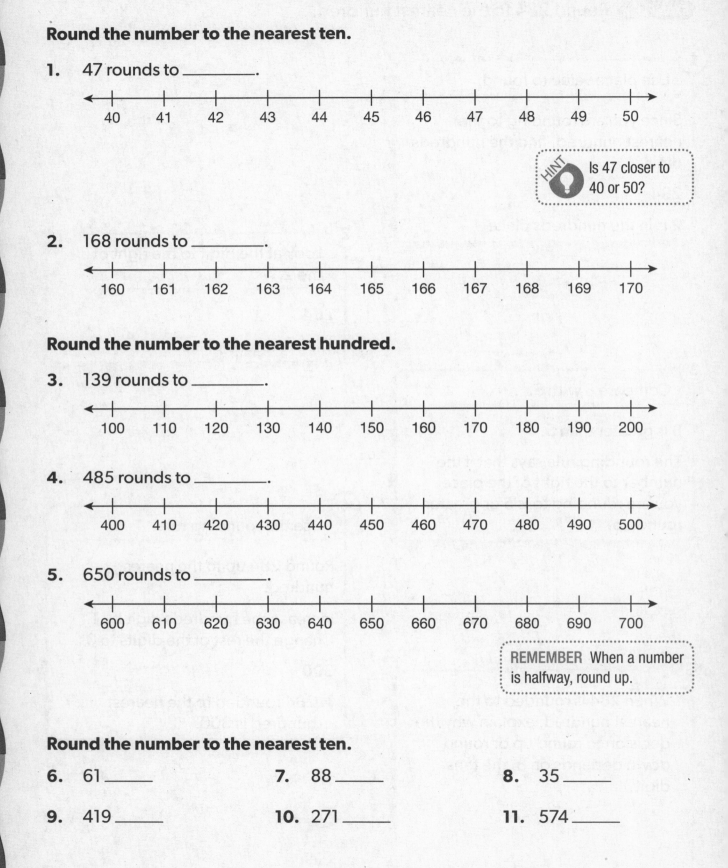

Number line: 40 41 42 43 44 45 46 47 48 49 50

HINT Is 47 closer to 40 or 50?

2. 168 rounds to _____.

Number line: 160 161 162 163 164 165 166 167 168 169 170

Round the number to the nearest hundred.

3. 139 rounds to _____.

Number line: 100 110 120 130 140 150 160 170 180 190 200

4. 485 rounds to _____.

Number line: 400 410 420 430 440 450 460 470 480 490 500

5. 650 rounds to _____.

Number line: 600 610 620 630 640 650 660 670 680 690 700

REMEMBER When a number is halfway, round up.

Round the number to the nearest ten.

6. 61 _____

7. 88 _____

8. 35 _____

9. 419 _____

10. 271 _____

11. 574 _____

Round the number to the nearest hundred.

12. 336 _____

13. 185 _____

14. 279 _____

15. 552 _____

16. 741 _____

17. 903 _____

Choose the best answer.

18. To the nearest ten, which number rounds to 80?

    A. 70

    B. 75

    C. 85

    D. 89

19. To the nearest hundred, which number rounds to 500?

    A. 438

    B. 449

    C. 540

    D. 555

Solve.

20. Ms. Torney's class has 28 students. To the nearest ten, how many students are in Ms. Torney's class?

_____

21. Kyle sold 213 raffle tickets. To the nearest hundred, about how many tickets did Kyle sell?

_____

22. **RECALL** When rounding a 2-digit number to the nearest ten, how do you know when to round up to the greater ten?

_____

_____

23. **ANALYZE** The number 495 rounds to 500 when rounded to the nearest ten and to the nearest hundred. Explain why this is true.

_____

_____

_____

Using Place Value to Add and Subtract Whole Numbers

UNDERSTAND When you **add** and **subtract** whole numbers, sometimes you need to **regroup**.

Subtract. 358 − 173

1

Use place-value models for 358. Show 3 hundreds, 5 tens, and 8 ones. Subtract 3 ones.

2

There are not enough tens in 358 to subtract 7 tens. Regroup 1 hundred as 10 tens. Then subtract 7 tens.

3

Subtract 1 hundred.

4

Count the models that are left.
There are 1 hundred, 8 tens, and 5 ones or 185 left.

▶ 358 − 173 = 185

← Connect

Subtract.

358 − 173

1 Write the problem in a place-value chart.
Subtract.
8 ones − 3 ones = 5 ones

	Hundreds	Tens	Ones
	3	5	**8**
−	1	7	**3**
			5

2 There are not enough tens to subtract.
Regroup 1 hundred as 10 tens.
Now there are 15 tens.
Subtract. 15 tens − 7 tens = 8 tens

	Hundreds	Tens	Ones
	2	**15**	
	3̶	5̶	8
−	1	7	3
		8	**5**

3 Subtract. 2 hundreds −
1 hundred = 1 hundred

	Hundreds	Tens	Ones
	2	15	
	3̶	5̶	8
−	1	7	3
	1	8	5

4 Find the **difference**.

There are 1 hundred, 8 tens, and 5 ones, or 185 left.

▶ 358 − 173 = 185

TRY

Subtract. 508 − 293

EXAMPLE A At the bakery, Steve made 145 blueberry muffins and 286 chocolate muffins. How many muffins did Steve make?

Add. $145 + 286 = \square$

1 Write the problem in a place-value chart.
Add. 5 ones + 6 ones = 11 ones
Regroup 11 ones as 1 ten 1 one.

	Hundreds	Tens	Ones
		1	
	1	4	5
+	2	8	6
			1

2 Add.
1 ten + 4 tens + 8 tens = 13 tens
Regroup 13 tens as 1 hundred 3 tens.

	Hundreds	Tens	Ones
	1	1	
	1	4	5
+	2	8	6
		3	1

3 Add. 1 hundred + 1 hundred + 2 hundreds = 4 hundreds

	Hundreds	Tens	Ones
	1	1	
	1	4	5
+	2	8	6
	4	3	1

4 Find the **sum**.

There are 4 hundreds, 3 tens, and 1 one, or 431.
The sum, $\square$, is 431.

▶ Steve made 431 muffins in all.

DISCUSS
Explain what the symbol $\square$ means in this problem.

EXAMPLE B Subtract. 744 − 498

1 Set up the problem. Line up the numbers by place value.

$$\begin{array}{r} 744 \\ -498 \\ \hline \end{array}$$

2 Subtract the ones.

Regroup 1 ten as 10 ones.
Now there are 14 ones.
Subtract. 14 ones − 8 ones = 6 ones

$$\begin{array}{r} {}^{3\ 14} \\ 7\cancel{4}\cancel{4} \\ -498 \\ \hline 6 \end{array}$$

3 Subtract the tens.

Regroup 1 hundred as 10 tens.
Now there are 13 tens.
Subtract. 13 tens − 9 tens = 4 tens

$$\begin{array}{r} {}^{13} \\ 6\ \cancel{3}\ 14 \\ \cancel{7}\cancel{4}\cancel{4} \\ -498 \\ \hline 46 \end{array}$$

4 Subtract the hundreds.

Subtract. 6 hundreds −
4 hundreds = 2 hundreds

$$\begin{array}{r} {}^{13} \\ 6\ 3\ 14 \\ \cancel{7}\cancel{4}\cancel{4} \\ -498 \\ \hline 246 \end{array}$$

5 Find the difference.

There are 2 hundreds, 4 tens, and 6 ones, or 246.

▶ 744 − 498 = 246

CHECK

Use addition to check your answer.

Addition and subtraction are **inverse operations**.

$$\begin{array}{r} 246 \\ +498 \\ \hline \end{array}$$ ← difference
← **subtrahend**
← This should match the **minuend**.

Practice

Do you need to regroup? Write *yes* or *no*.

1. 217 + 252

2. 582 − 136

3. 345 − 123

_____   _____   _____

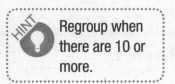
HINT Regroup when there are 10 or more.

Fill in the numbers in the boxes to complete the addition or subtraction.

4.

Hundreds	Tens	Ones
7	4	6
+ 1	5	2
☐	☐	8

5.

Hundreds	Tens	Ones
1	1	
4	5	1
+ 2	8	9
☐	☐	☐

6.

Hundreds	Tens	Ones
☐	☐	
3	9	7
+ 3	4	6
☐	☐	☐

7.

Hundreds	Tens	Ones
6	3	8
− 3	1	5
☐	2	☐

8.

Hundreds	Tens	Ones
	6	12
5	7̶	2̶
− 2	6	6
☐	☐	☐

9.

Hundreds	Tens	Ones
	☐	
☐	☐	☐
7̶	3̶	4
− 4	7	8
☐	☐	☐

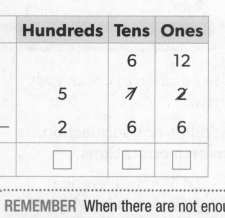

REMEMBER When there are not enough ones to subtract, regroup from the column to the left.

Add or subtract.

10. 257
    $+138$

11. 573
    $+263$

12. 362
    -171

13. 426
    -289

14. 722
    -365

15. 583
    $+285$

16. 137
    $+653$

17. 300
    -175

Choose the best answer.

18. Which can you use to check the difference of $362 - 185$?

    A. $362 + 177$

    B. $185 - 177$

    C. $362 + 185$

    D. $177 + 185$

19. Which can you use to check the difference of $523 - 176$?

    A. $347 + 176$

    B. $523 + 347$

    C. $347 - 176$

    D. $523 + 176$

Solve.

20. John ate a cheeseburger with 475 calories and fries with 220 calories. How many calories did John eat?

    _____

21. There are 365 days in a year. The students are in school for 187 days a year. How many days are the students not in school?

    _____

22. **RECALL** Explain the steps you would use to solve $422 - 167$.

    _____

    _____

    _____

23. **CREATE** Use $116 + 205 = \Box$ to write a real world problem.

    _____

    _____

    _____

12 Using Place Value to Multiply by Multiples of 10

UNDERSTAND Use place-value models to help you multiply by **multiples** of 10. The multiples of 10 are 10, 20, 30, 40, and so on.

Multiply. 5 × 30

1 Show 5 groups of 3 tens.

2 Group 10 tens as 1 hundred.

3 Count the models.

There are 1 hundred and 5 tens, or 150.

▶ 5 × 30 = 150

⊏ Connect

Multiply.

5 × 30

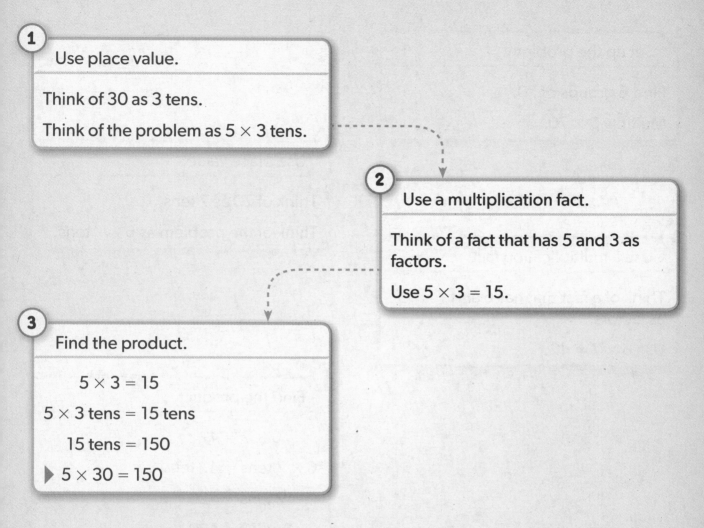

1 Use place value.

Think of 30 as 3 tens.

Think of the problem as 5 × 3 tens.

2 Use a multiplication fact.

Think of a fact that has 5 and 3 as factors.

Use 5 × 3 = 15.

3 Find the product.

5 × 3 = 15

5 × 3 tens = 15 tens

15 tens = 150

▶ 5 × 30 = 150

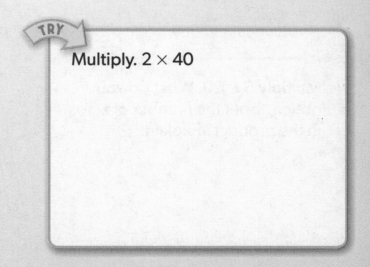

TRY

Multiply. 2 × 40

EXAMPLE Carol ordered 6 boxes of pencils. Each box has 70 pencils. How many pencils did Carol order?

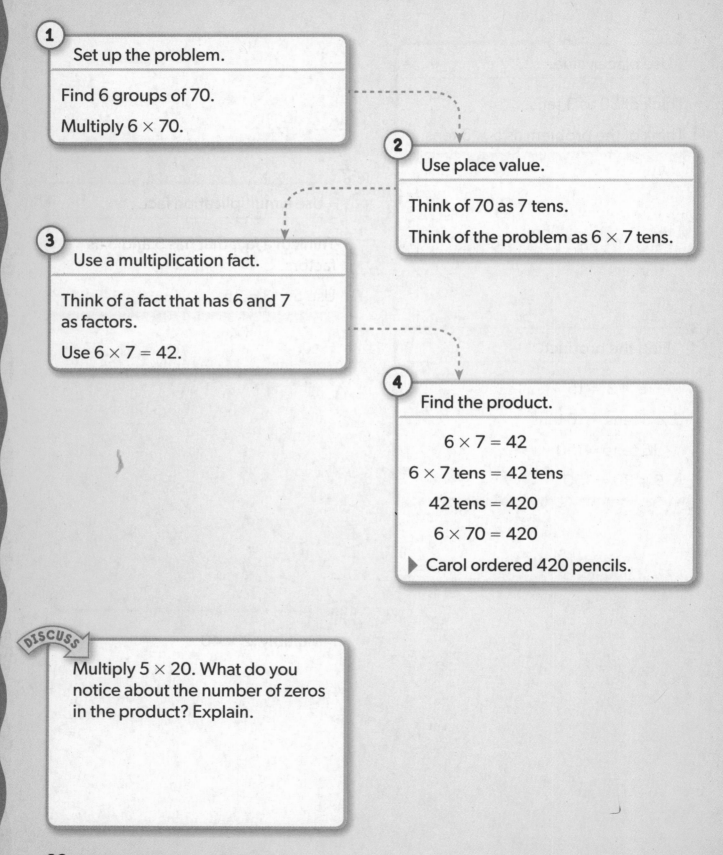

1

Set up the problem.

Find 6 groups of 70.

Multiply 6 × 70.

2

Use place value.

Think of 70 as 7 tens.

Think of the problem as 6 × 7 tens.

3

Use a multiplication fact.

Think of a fact that has 6 and 7 as factors.

Use 6 × 7 = 42.

4

Find the product.

6 × 7 = 42

6 × 7 tens = 42 tens

42 tens = 420

6 × 70 = 420

▶ Carol ordered 420 pencils.

DISCUSS

Multiply 5 × 20. What do you notice about the number of zeros in the product? Explain.

Mystery Number

Find the value of the first shape in each puzzle.
Use that value in the next line.
Continue until you find each mystery number.

1. $8 \times 30 = \square$

$\square + \square = \bigcirc$

$\bigcirc + \bigcirc = \triangle$

$\triangle$ = mystery number

The mystery number is _____.

2. $2 \times \bigcirc = 180$

$\bigcirc + \bigcirc = \square$

$\square + \square = \triangle$

$\triangle$ = mystery number

The mystery number is _____.

3. $\square \times 4 = 120$

$\square + \square = \triangle$

$\triangle + \triangle = \bigcirc$

$\bigcirc$ = mystery number

The mystery number is _____.

4. $7 \times \triangle = 140$

$\triangle + \triangle = \bigcirc$

$\bigcirc + \bigcirc = \square$

$\square$ = mystery number

The mystery number is _____.

5. $\bigcirc \times 60 = 300$

$\bigcirc + \bigcirc = \square$

$\square - \square = \triangle$

$\triangle$ = mystery number

The mystery number is _____.

6. $40 \times \square = 360$

$\square \times \square = \triangle$

$\triangle + \triangle = \bigcirc$

$\bigcirc$ = mystery number

The mystery number is _____.

Practice

Write an equation that the models show.

1.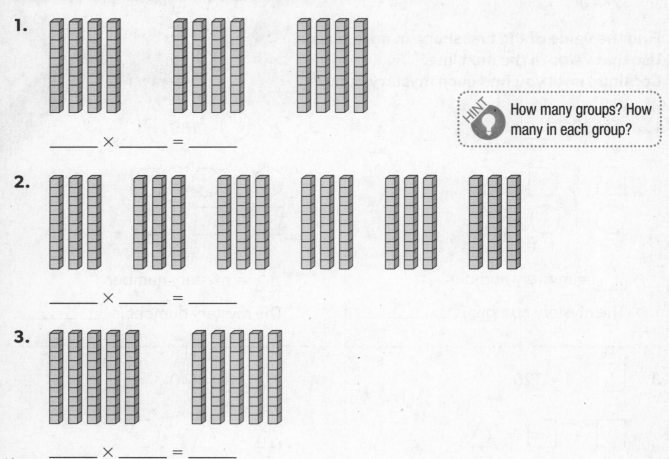

_____ × _____ = _____

HINT
How many groups? How many in each group?

2.

_____ × _____ = _____

3.

_____ × _____ = _____

Find the multiplication fact that you would use. Then find the product.

4. 2 × 80

Use the fact: 2 × 8 = _____

2 × 80 = _____

5. 4 × 70

Use the fact: _____ × _____ = _____

4 × 70 = _____

6. 9 × 50

Use the fact: _____ × _____ = _____

9 × 50 = _____

7. 70 × 9

Use the fact: _____ × _____ = _____

70 × 9 = _____

REMEMBER The order of the factors does not change the product.

Multiply.

8. $3 \times 50 =$ _____

9. $6 \times 60 =$ _____

10. $5 \times 80 =$ _____

11. $30 \times 7 =$ _____

12. $40 \times 8 =$ _____

13. $60 \times 2 =$ _____

Complete the multiplication sentences.

14. $3 \times$ _____ $= 270$

_____ $\times 3 = 270$

15. $6 \times$ _____ $= 300$

_____ $\times 6 = 300$

Choose the best answer.

16. Which basic fact can you use to help multiply 7×80?

  A. $7 \times 3 = 21$

  B. $8 \times 10 = 80$

  C. $7 \times 8 = 56$

  D. $8 \times 6 = 48$

17. Which basic fact can you use to multiply 20×9?

  A. $9 \times 2 = 18$

  B. $2 \times 8 = 16$

  C. $8 \times 9 = 72$

  D. $2 \times 5 = 10$

Solve.

18. An MP3 player costs $50. Ms. Roberts bought 4 MP3 players. How much did Ms. Roberts spend in all?

_____

19. There are 30 tennis players on the courts. Each player needs 3 tennis balls. How many tennis balls are needed?

_____

20. (DESCRIBE) Explain how you would multiply 6×80.

_____

_____

_____

21. (CREATE) Use $2 \times 70 = \boxed{}$ to write a real-world problem.

_____

_____

_____

Review

Round the number to the nearest ten.

1. 62 rounds to _____.

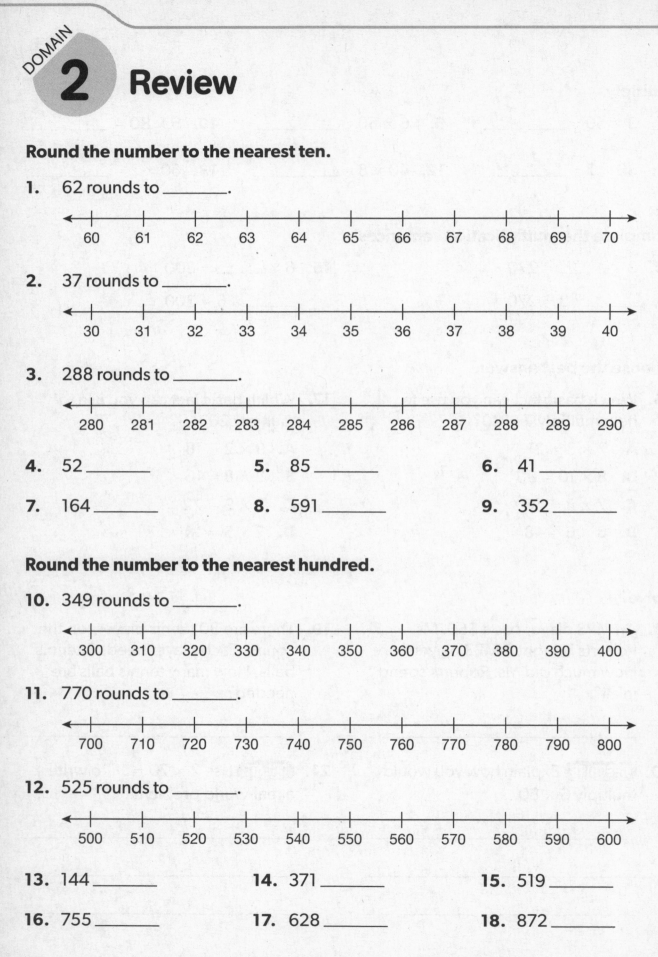

2. 37 rounds to _____.

3. 288 rounds to _____.

4. 52 _____   5. 85 _____   6. 41 _____

7. 164 _____   8. 591 _____   9. 352 _____

Round the number to the nearest hundred.

10. 349 rounds to _____.

11. 770 rounds to _____.

12. 525 rounds to _____.

13. 144 _____   14. 371 _____   15. 519 _____

16. 755 _____   17. 628 _____   18. 872 _____

Add or subtract.

19. $\begin{array}{r} 326 \\ +213 \\ \hline \end{array}$

20. $\begin{array}{r} 468 \\ +171 \\ \hline \end{array}$

21. $\begin{array}{r} 495 \\ +257 \\ \hline \end{array}$

22. $\begin{array}{r} 575 \\ -242 \\ \hline \end{array}$

23. $\begin{array}{r} 618 \\ -377 \\ \hline \end{array}$

24. $\begin{array}{r} 814 \\ -246 \\ \hline \end{array}$

Choose the best answer.

25. Which can you use to check the difference of $279 - 133$?

   A. $279 + 133$

   B. $146 - 133$

   C. $279 + 146$

   D. $146 + 133$

26. Which can you use to check the difference of $648 - 265$?

   A. $383 + 265$

   B. $648 + 265$

   C. $383 - 265$

   D. $265 + 265$

27. Which multiplication fact can you use to find the product of 5×40?

   A. $4 \times 3 = 12$

   B. $4 \times 4 = 16$

   C. $5 \times 4 = 20$

   D. $5 \times 6 = 30$

28. Which multiplication fact can you use to find the product of 7×50?

   A. $5 \times 6 = 30$

   B. $6 \times 7 = 42$

   C. $7 \times 4 = 28$

   D. $7 \times 5 = 35$

Multiply.

29. $2 \times 90 = \underline{\hspace{2cm}}$

30. $9 \times 80 = \underline{\hspace{2cm}}$

31. $7 \times 30 = \underline{\hspace{2cm}}$

32. $3 \times 60 = \underline{\hspace{2cm}}$

33. $6 \times 50 = \underline{\hspace{2cm}}$

34. $4 \times 80 = \underline{\hspace{2cm}}$

35. $10 \times 8 = \underline{\hspace{2cm}}$

36. $20 \times 9 = \underline{\hspace{2cm}}$

37. $50 \times 4 = \underline{\hspace{2cm}}$

Solve.

38. Colleen counted 227 cars in the parking lot. To the nearest hundred, how many cars did Colleen count in the parking lot?

_____

39. Miles scored 174 points in a game. Brenda scored 83 more points than Miles. How many points did Brenda score?

_____

40. Carter sold 528 raffle tickets. Erin sold 395 tickets. How many more tickets did Carter sell than Erin?

_____

41. Each classroom has 20 students. How many students are in 7 classrooms?

_____

42. A company has 638 full-time workers and 175 part-time workers. During the holidays, the company hires an additional 93 workers. How many workers in all does the company have during the holidays? Solve the problem. Use estimation to check that your answer makes sense.

The company has _____ workers during the holidays.

43. Kayla bought 4 boxes of gold beads. Each box has 50 gold beads. She also bought 3 boxes of silver beads. Each box has 20 silver beads. How many more gold beads than silver beads did Kayla buy?

Kayla bought _____ more gold beads than silver beads.

44. CREATE Use $4 \times 50 = \square$ to write a real world problem.

_____

_____

shopping trip

The Drew family has $850 to spend on things they need for their home. Here are some items the Drew family would like to have.

Loveseat $375   Floor Lamp $128   Chair $80   Table $256   20-inch TV $215

1. The Drew family wants to buy the loveseat and the floor lamp. Estimate to find about how much they will spend on the loveseat and the floor lamp. Show your work.

   The loveseat and floor lamp cost about _____.

2. How much more does the TV cost than the floor lamp? Show your work.

   The TV costs _____ more than the floor lamp.

3. How much will the table and 4 chairs cost? Show your work.

   The table and 4 chairs cost _____.

4. What is the greatest amount of their money that the Drew family can spend? List the items they can buy and the total amount they will spend. Show your work.

   _____

   _____

Grade 2

Grade 3

Grade 4

Grade 4 NF

Extend understanding of fraction equivalence and ordering.

Build fractions from unit fractions by applying and extending previous understandings of operations on whole numbers.

Understand decimal notation for fractions, and compare decimal fractions.

Grade 2 MD

Relate addition and subtraction to length.

Grade 3 NF

Develop understanding of fractions as numbers.

Grade 2 G

Reason with shapes and their attributes

Grade 4 MD

Solve problems involving measurement and conversion of measurements from a larger unit to a smaller unit.

Represent and interpret data.

Domain 3
Number and Operations–Fractions

13 Understanding Fractions

UNDERSTAND A **fraction** names part of a whole.

How can you show the fraction $\frac{1}{6}$?

1

Think about a whole pie.

2

The 6 in the fraction means the number of pieces.
Divide the pie into 6 equal pieces.

Equal pieces means pieces that are the same size.

3

The 1 in the fraction means one of the pieces.
Separate out 1 of the 6 pieces.

▶ You can draw a picture to show $\frac{1}{6}$.
First divide a whole into 6 equal parts.
Then show 1 of the parts.

⊷ Connect

How can you show the fraction $\frac{1}{6}$?

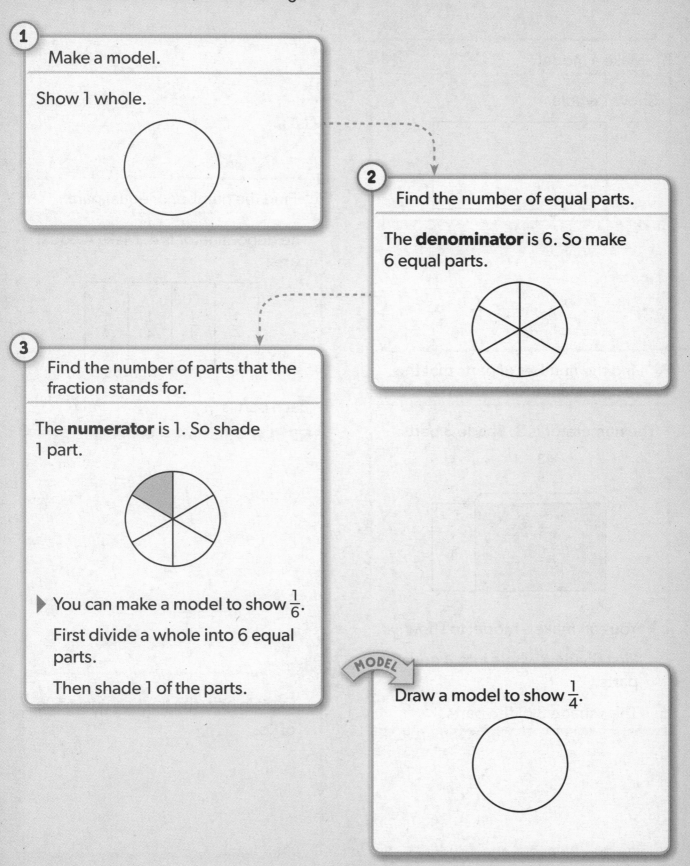

1 Make a model.

Show 1 whole.

2 Find the number of equal parts.

The **denominator** is 6. So make 6 equal parts.

3 Find the number of parts that the fraction stands for.

The **numerator** is 1. So shade 1 part.

▶ You can make a model to show $\frac{1}{6}$.

First divide a whole into 6 equal parts.

Then shade 1 of the parts.

MODEL

Draw a model to show $\frac{1}{4}$.

EXAMPLE A How can you show the fraction $\frac{3}{4}$?

1

Make a model.

Show 1 whole.

2

Find the number of equal parts.

The denominator is 4. Make 4 equal parts.

$\frac{1}{4}$	$\frac{1}{4}$	$\frac{1}{4}$	$\frac{1}{4}$

Each part is $\frac{1}{4}$.

3

Find the number of parts that the fraction stands for.

The numerator is 3. Shade 3 parts.

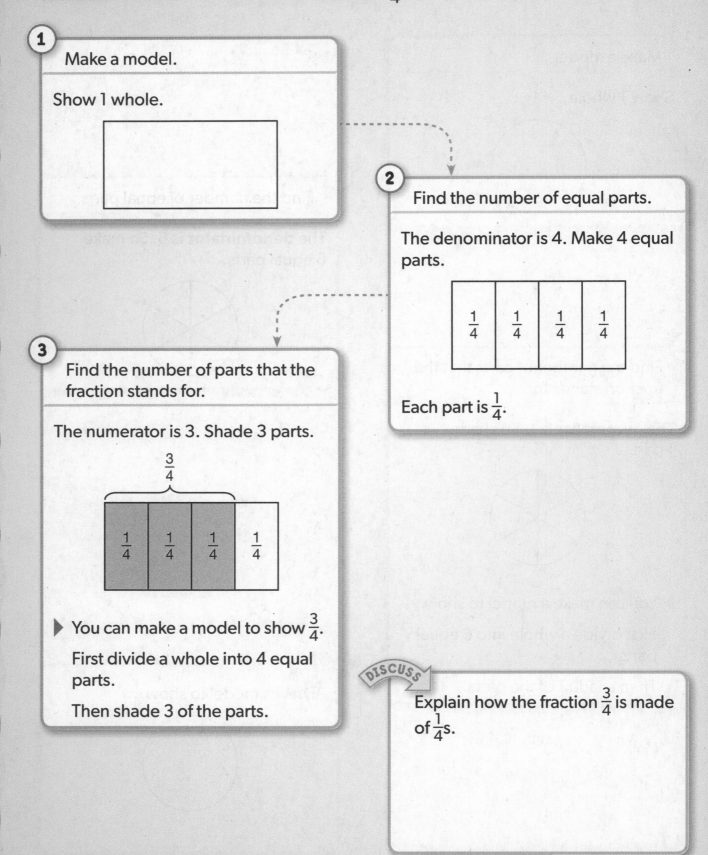

$\frac{3}{4}$

$\frac{1}{4}$	$\frac{1}{4}$	$\frac{1}{4}$	$\frac{1}{4}$

▶ You can make a model to show $\frac{3}{4}$.

First divide a whole into 4 equal parts.

Then shade 3 of the parts.

DISCUSS

Explain how the fraction $\frac{3}{4}$ is made of $\frac{1}{4}$s.

EXAMPLE B What part of the square is shaded?

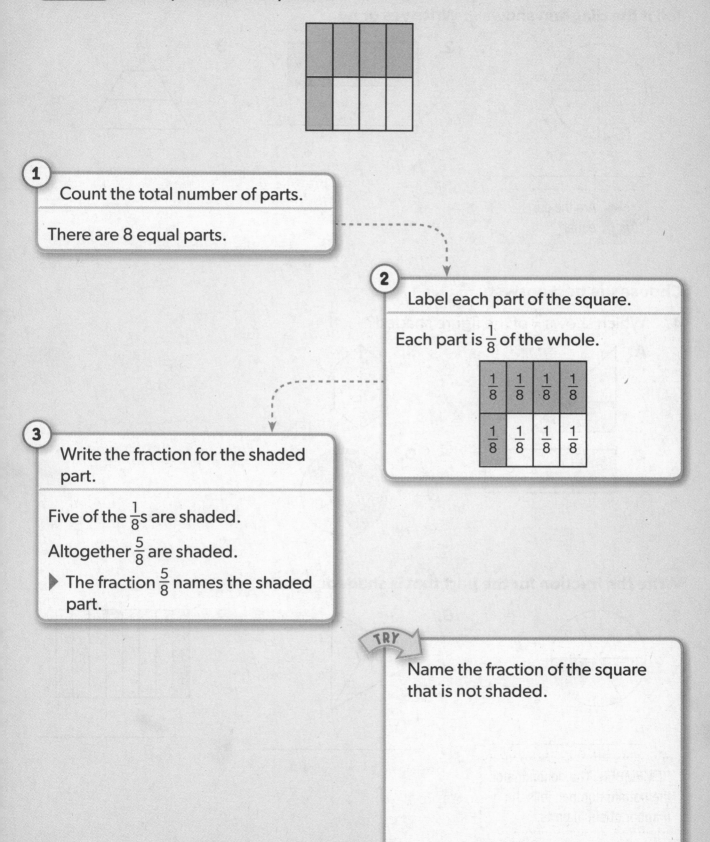

1

Count the total number of parts.

There are 8 equal parts.

2

Label each part of the square.

Each part is $\frac{1}{8}$ of the whole.

| $\frac{1}{8}$ | $\frac{1}{8}$ | $\frac{1}{8}$ | $\frac{1}{8}$ |
| $\frac{1}{8}$ | $\frac{1}{8}$ | $\frac{1}{8}$ | $\frac{1}{8}$ |

3

Write the fraction for the shaded part.

Five of the $\frac{1}{8}$s are shaded.

Altogether $\frac{5}{8}$ are shaded.

▶ The fraction $\frac{5}{8}$ names the shaded part.

TRY

Name the fraction of the square that is not shaded.

Practice

Tell if the diagram shows $\frac{1}{3}$. Write *yes* or *no*.

1.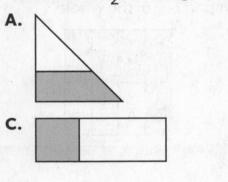

_____

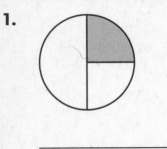
HINT Are the parts equal?

2.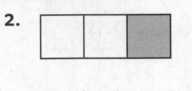

_____

3.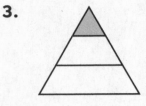

_____

Choose the best answer.

4. Which shows $\frac{1}{2}$ of the figure shaded?

A.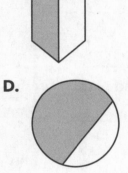

B.

C.

D.

Write the fraction for the part that is shaded.

5.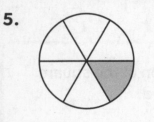

_____

6.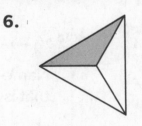

_____

7.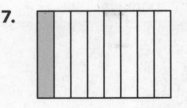

_____

REMEMBER The denominator, the bottom number, tells the number of equal parts.

Shade the figure to show the fraction.

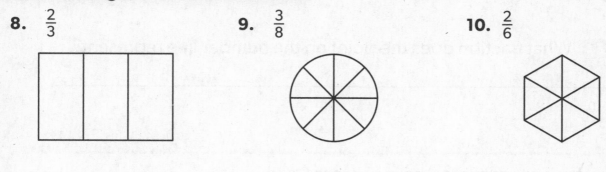

8. $\frac{2}{3}$

9. $\frac{3}{8}$

10. $\frac{2}{6}$

Write the fraction for the part that is shaded.

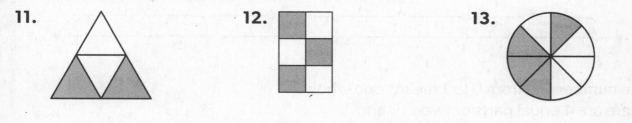

11.

12.

13.

_____   _____   _____

Solve.

14. Jill baked a cake and cut it into 6 equal pieces. She gave 1 piece to her neighbor. What fraction of the cake did Jill give to her neighbor?

_____

15. A pizza had 8 slices. Yung, Nina, and Betty each ate a slice. What fraction of the pizza did they eat?

_____

16. **ILLUSTRATE** Draw a diagram to show a whole divided into 3 equal parts. Label each part with a fraction.

17. **DESCRIBE** A figure has 4 equal parts. All of the parts are shaded. What is the fraction that shows the shaded part? Explain your answer.

_____

_____

_____

14 Representing Fractions on a Number Line

EXAMPLE A What fraction does the point on the number line represent?

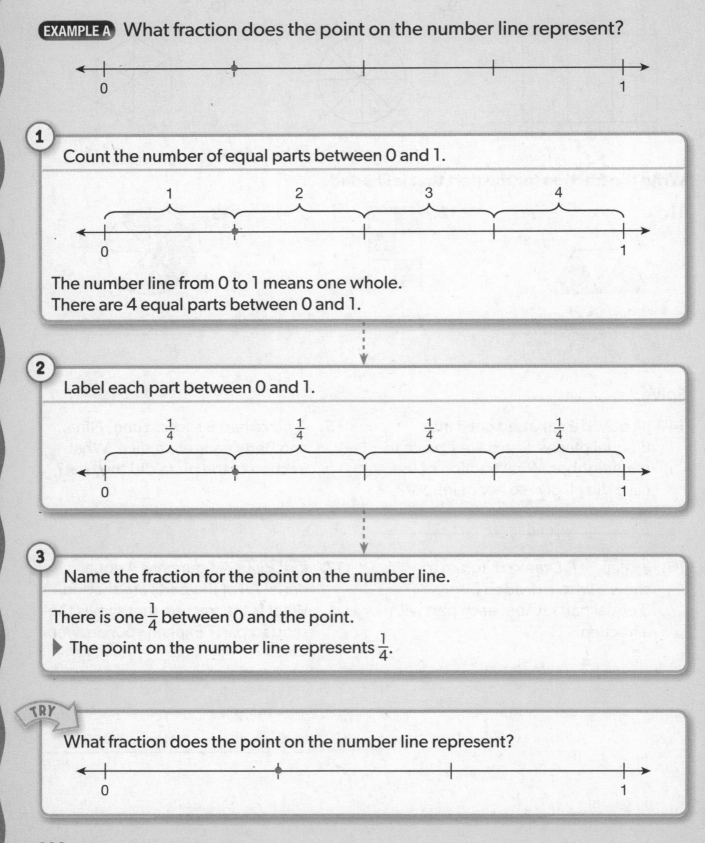

1

Count the number of equal parts between 0 and 1.

The number line from 0 to 1 means one whole.
There are 4 equal parts between 0 and 1.

2

Label each part between 0 and 1.

3

Name the fraction for the point on the number line.

There is one $\frac{1}{4}$ between 0 and the point.

▶ The point on the number line represents $\frac{1}{4}$.

TRY

What fraction does the point on the number line represent?

EXAMPLE B What fraction does the point on the number line represent?

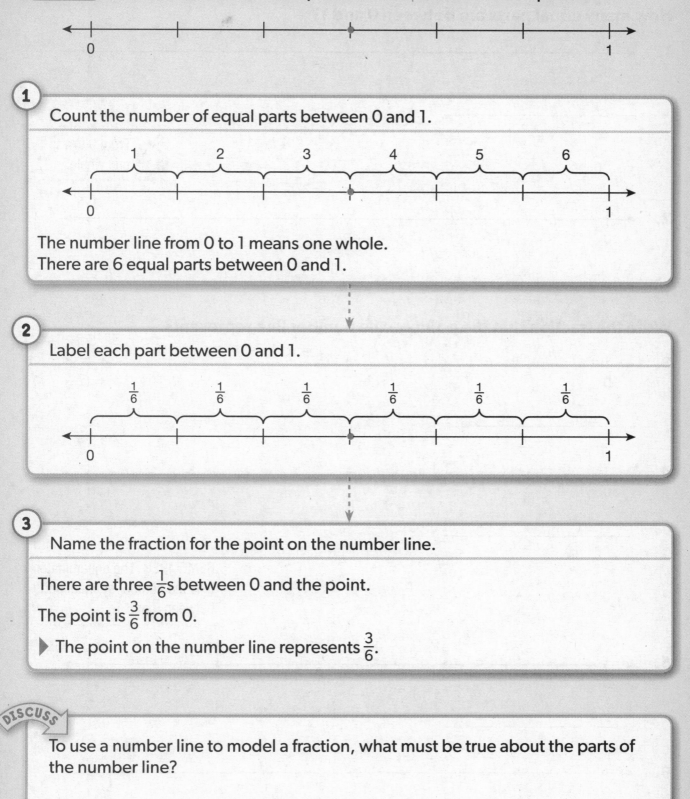

1 Count the number of equal parts between 0 and 1.

The number line from 0 to 1 means one whole.
There are 6 equal parts between 0 and 1.

2 Label each part between 0 and 1.

3 Name the fraction for the point on the number line.

There are three $\frac{1}{6}$s between 0 and the point.

The point is $\frac{3}{6}$ from 0.

▶ The point on the number line represents $\frac{3}{6}$.

DISCUSS

To use a number line to model a fraction, what must be true about the parts of the number line?

Practice

How many equal parts are between 0 and 1?

1.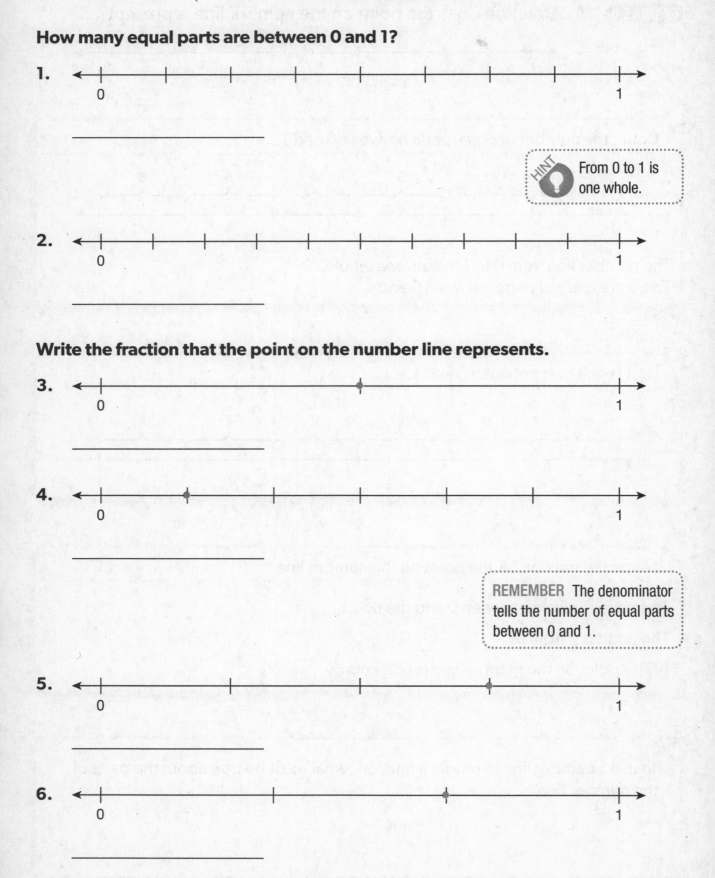

_____

HINT From 0 to 1 is one whole.

2.

_____

Write the fraction that the point on the number line represents.

3.

_____

4.

_____

REMEMBER The denominator tells the number of equal parts between 0 and 1.

5.

_____

6.

_____

Choose the best answer.

7. Which number line has a point on $\frac{3}{8}$?

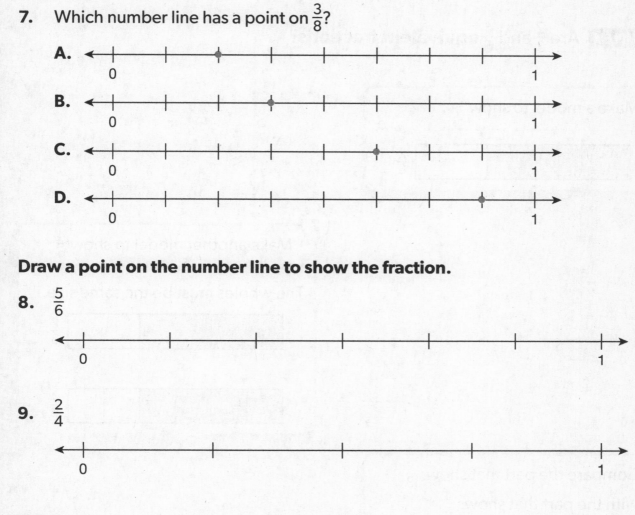

A. 0   1

B. 0   1

C. 0   1

D. 0   1

Draw a point on the number line to show the fraction.

8. $\frac{5}{6}$

0   1

9. $\frac{2}{4}$

0   1

Solve.

10. **RECALL** Explain how you can find the fraction $\frac{1}{6}$ on a number line.

_____

_____

11. **COMPARE** How far is a point at $\frac{2}{8}$ from a point at $\frac{7}{8}$? Explain or make a diagram to show your answer.

_____

_____

LESSON 15 Understanding Equivalent Fractions

EXAMPLE A Are $\frac{2}{3}$ and $\frac{4}{6}$ **equivalent fractions**?

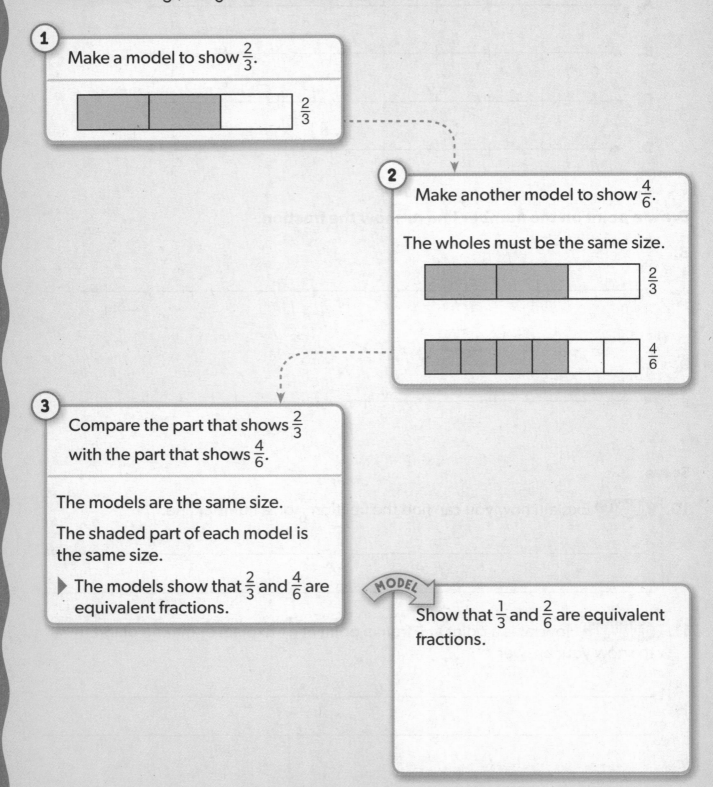

1 Make a model to show $\frac{2}{3}$.

$\frac{2}{3}$

2 Make another model to show $\frac{4}{6}$.

The wholes must be the same size.

$\frac{2}{3}$

$\frac{4}{6}$

3 Compare the part that shows $\frac{2}{3}$ with the part that shows $\frac{4}{6}$.

The models are the same size.

The shaded part of each model is the same size.

▶ The models show that $\frac{2}{3}$ and $\frac{4}{6}$ are equivalent fractions.

MODEL
Show that $\frac{1}{3}$ and $\frac{2}{6}$ are equivalent fractions.

EXAMPLE B Are $\frac{2}{4}$ and $\frac{3}{6}$ equivalent fractions?

1

Draw a number line in fourths. Find $\frac{2}{4}$.

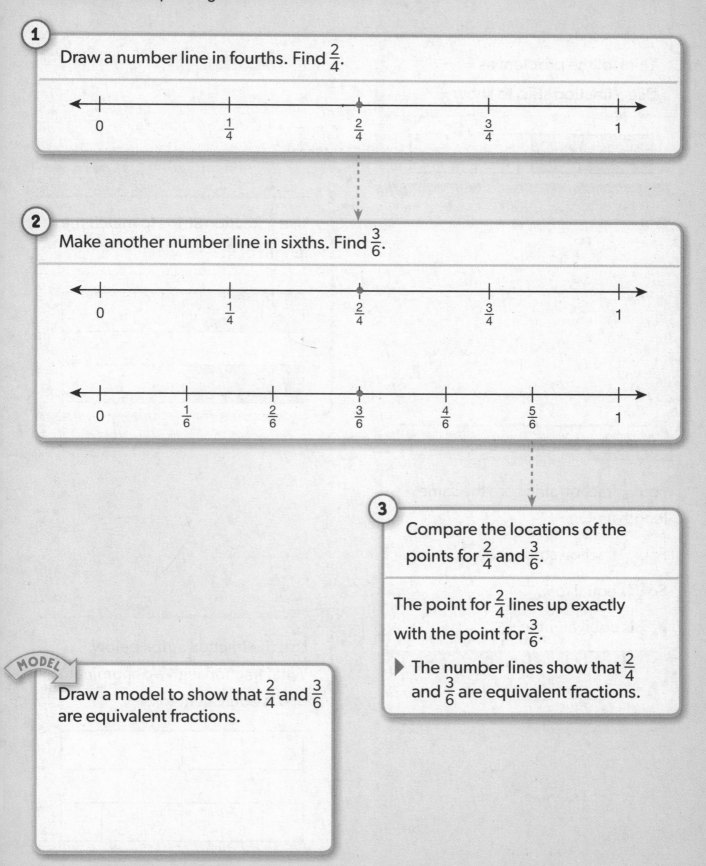

2

Make another number line in sixths. Find $\frac{3}{6}$.

3

Compare the locations of the points for $\frac{2}{4}$ and $\frac{3}{6}$.

The point for $\frac{2}{4}$ lines up exactly with the point for $\frac{3}{6}$.

▶ The number lines show that $\frac{2}{4}$ and $\frac{3}{6}$ are equivalent fractions.

MODEL

Draw a model to show that $\frac{2}{4}$ and $\frac{3}{6}$ are equivalent fractions.

EXAMPLE C What fraction with a denominator of 8 is equivalent to $\frac{1}{2}$?

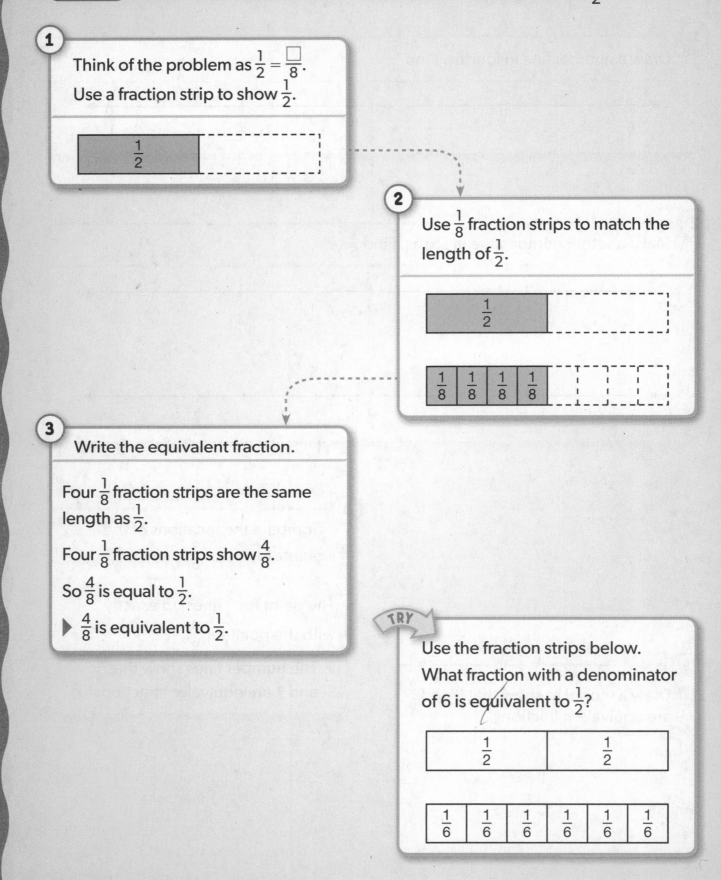

1

Think of the problem as $\frac{1}{2} = \frac{\square}{8}$.
Use a fraction strip to show $\frac{1}{2}$.

| $\frac{1}{2}$ | |

2

Use $\frac{1}{8}$ fraction strips to match the length of $\frac{1}{2}$.

| $\frac{1}{2}$ | |

| $\frac{1}{8}$ | $\frac{1}{8}$ | $\frac{1}{8}$ | $\frac{1}{8}$ | | | | |

3

Write the equivalent fraction.

Four $\frac{1}{8}$ fraction strips are the same length as $\frac{1}{2}$.

Four $\frac{1}{8}$ fraction strips show $\frac{4}{8}$.

So $\frac{4}{8}$ is equal to $\frac{1}{2}$.

▶ $\frac{4}{8}$ is equivalent to $\frac{1}{2}$.

TRY

Use the fraction strips below.
What fraction with a denominator of 6 is equivalent to $\frac{1}{2}$?

| $\frac{1}{2}$ | $\frac{1}{2}$ |

| $\frac{1}{6}$ | $\frac{1}{6}$ | $\frac{1}{6}$ | $\frac{1}{6}$ | $\frac{1}{6}$ | $\frac{1}{6}$ |

EXAMPLE D Name a fraction with a denominator of 3 that is equal to 1.

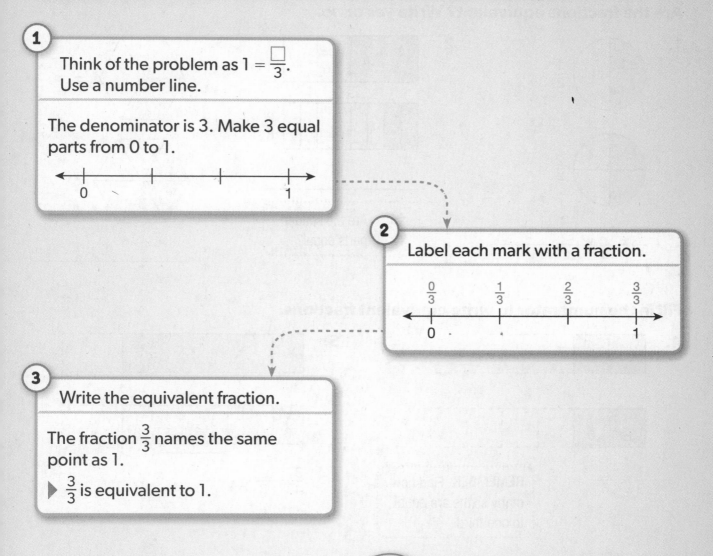

1

Think of the problem as $1 = \frac{\square}{3}$.
Use a number line.

The denominator is 3. Make 3 equal parts from 0 to 1.

0   1

2

Label each mark with a fraction.

$\frac{0}{3}$ $\frac{1}{3}$ $\frac{2}{3}$ $\frac{3}{3}$

0   1

3

Write the equivalent fraction.

The fraction $\frac{3}{3}$ names the same point as 1.

▶ $\frac{3}{3}$ is equivalent to 1.

CHECK

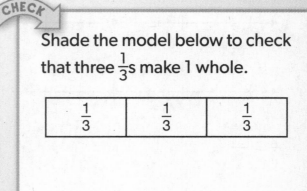

Shade the model below to check that three $\frac{1}{3}$s make 1 whole.

$\frac{1}{3}$	$\frac{1}{3}$	$\frac{1}{3}$

Practice

Are the fractions equivalent? Write *yes* or *no*.

1.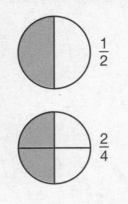

$\frac{1}{2}$

$\frac{2}{4}$

_____

2.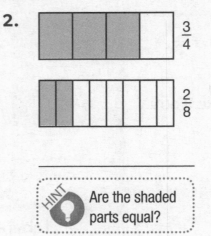

$\frac{3}{4}$

$\frac{2}{8}$

_____

> **HINT** Are the shaded parts equal?

3.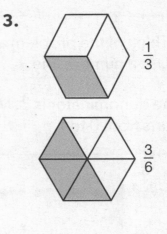

$\frac{1}{3}$

$\frac{3}{6}$

_____

Fill in the numerator to write equivalent fractions.

4.

| $\frac{1}{3}$ | | |

| $\frac{1}{6}$ | $\frac{1}{6}$ | | | |

$\frac{1}{3} = \frac{\square}{6}$

> **REMEMBER** Find how many sixths are equal to one third.

5.

| $\frac{1}{4}$ | $\frac{1}{4}$ | $\frac{1}{4}$ | |

| $\frac{1}{8}$ | $\frac{1}{8}$ | $\frac{1}{8}$ | $\frac{1}{8}$ | $\frac{1}{8}$ | $\frac{1}{8}$ | | |

$\frac{3}{4} = \frac{\square}{8}$

6.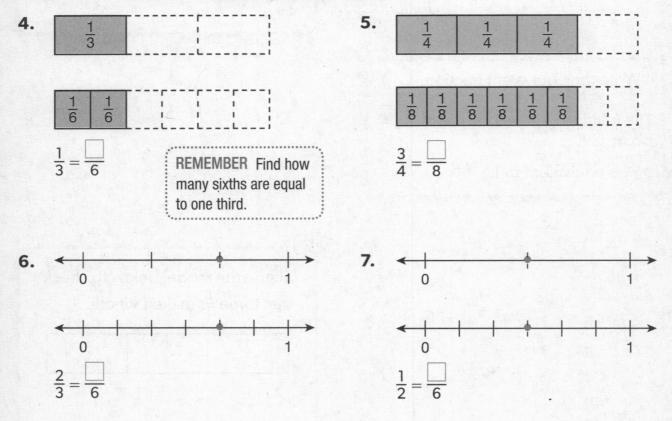

$\frac{2}{3} = \frac{\square}{6}$

7.

$\frac{1}{2} = \frac{\square}{6}$

Use the models to write equivalent fractions.

8.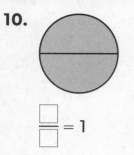

_____ = _____

9.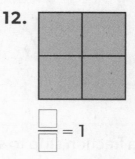

_____ = _____

Use the model to write a fraction for 1 whole.

10.

$\frac{\square}{\square} = 1$

11.

$\frac{\square}{\square} = 1$

12.

$\frac{\square}{\square} = 1$

Choose the best answer.

13. Which fraction is equivalent to 5?

   A. $\frac{5}{5}$

   B. $\frac{5}{1}$

   C. $\frac{1}{5}$

   D. $\frac{1}{1}$

14. Which fraction is equivalent to 8?

   A. $\frac{4}{4}$

   B. $\frac{8}{8}$

   C. $\frac{1}{8}$

   D. $\frac{8}{1}$

Solve.

15. **IDENTIFY** Write a fraction that is equivalent to 6. Explain why the fraction is equivalent to 6.

_____

_____

16. **DEMONSTRATE** Use the number line to show that 1 whole is equivalent to a fraction with a denominator of 8. Plot the point and label the fractions.

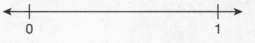

16 Comparing Fractions

UNDERSTAND When you compare fractions, the wholes that you compare must be the same size.

Which is the greater fraction, $\frac{1}{2}$ or $\frac{1}{3}$?

1

Use a fraction strip to show $\frac{1}{2}$.

| $\frac{1}{2}$ |

2

Use a fraction strip to show $\frac{1}{3}$.
Make sure that the wholes are the same size.

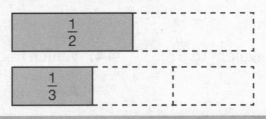

3

Compare the fraction strips.

The fraction strip for $\frac{1}{2}$ is longer than the fraction strip for $\frac{1}{3}$.

So, $\frac{1}{2}$ is greater than $\frac{1}{3}$.

▶ $\frac{1}{2}$ is the greater fraction.

Connect

Which is the greater fraction, $\frac{1}{2}$ or $\frac{1}{3}$?

1

Compare the numerators.

The numerator of each fraction is 1.

The numerators are the same.

2

Compare the denominators.

The denominators are 2 and 3.

The denominators are different.

3

Compare the fractions by comparing the denominators.

Halves are larger than thirds.

So, 1 half is larger than 1 third.

$\frac{1}{2}$ is greater than $\frac{1}{3}$

▶ $\frac{1}{2}$ is the greater fraction.

CHECK

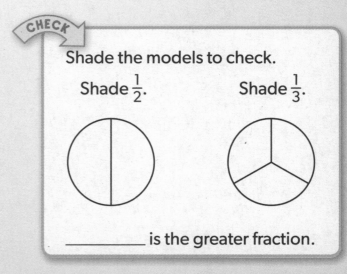

Shade the models to check.

Shade $\frac{1}{2}$.   Shade $\frac{1}{3}$.

_____ is the greater fraction.

EXAMPLE A Which is the greater fraction, $\frac{2}{8}$ or $\frac{5}{8}$?

1

Compare the numerators.

The numerators are 2 and 5.

The numerators are different.

2

Compare the denominators.

The denominator of each fraction is 8.

The denominators are the same.

3

Compare the fractions by comparing the numerators.

Each whole is divided into 8 equal parts.

2 parts is less than 5 parts, so

2 eighths is less than 5 eighths.

$\frac{2}{8}$ is less than $\frac{5}{8}$.

▶ $\frac{5}{8}$ is the greater fraction.

CHECK

Shade the models to check.

Shade $\frac{2}{8}$.

Shade $\frac{5}{8}$.

_____ is the greater fraction.

EXAMPLE B Compare the fractions. Use >, <, or =.

$\frac{3}{4}$ ◯ $\frac{1}{4}$

1

Compare the numerators.

The numerators are 3 and 1.

The numerators are different.

2

Compare the denominators.

The denominator of each fraction is 4.

The denominators are the same.

3

Compare the fractions by comparing the numerators.

Each whole is divided into 4 equal parts.

3 parts is more than 1 part, so 3 fourths is greater than 1 fourth.

$\frac{3}{4}$ is greater than $\frac{1}{4}$.

4

Use a symbol to compare.

Choose the correct symbol.

> means is greater than.

< means is less than.

▶ $\frac{3}{4}$ ⟨>⟩ $\frac{1}{4}$

CHECK

Shade the models to check.

Shade $\frac{3}{4}$.

Shade $\frac{1}{4}$.

$\frac{3}{4}$ ◯ $\frac{1}{4}$

EXAMPLE C Compare the fractions. Use $>$, $<$, or $=$.

$$\frac{2}{6} \bigcirc \frac{2}{3}$$

1

Compare the numerators.

The numerator of each fraction is 2.

The numerators are the same.

2

Compare the denominators.

The denominators are 6 and 3.

The denominators are different.

3

Compare the fractions by comparing the denominators.

Sixths are smaller than thirds, so 2 sixths is less than 2 thirds.

$\frac{2}{6}$ is less than $\frac{2}{3}$.

4

Use a symbol to compare.

Choose the correct symbol.

$>$ means is greater than.

$<$ means is less than.

▶ $\frac{2}{6} \bigcirc< \frac{2}{3}$

CHECK

Use number lines to check.

Find $\frac{2}{6}$ and $\frac{2}{3}$ on the number lines.

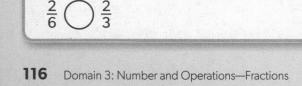

$$0 \quad \frac{1}{6} \quad \frac{2}{6} \quad \frac{3}{6} \quad \frac{4}{6} \quad \frac{5}{6} \quad 1$$

$$0 \qquad \frac{1}{3} \qquad \frac{2}{3} \qquad 1$$

Which of the fractions is closer to 0? _____

$$\frac{2}{6} \bigcirc \frac{2}{3}$$

Find the Greater Fraction

Circle the greater fraction in each box.

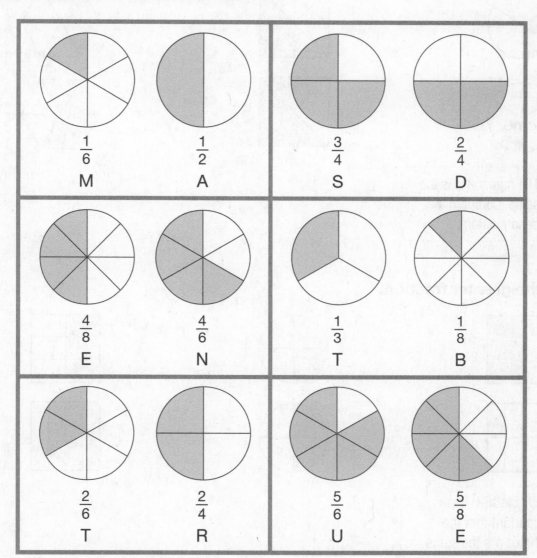

Write the letters that are below the fractions you circled.

_____ _____ _____ _____ _____

Unscramble the letters to discover the word.

Can you name the planet that has nine rings? It is the second largest planet in our solar system. It is the sixth planet from the sun. What planet is it?

_____ _____ _____ _____ _____

Practice

Circle the lesser fraction.

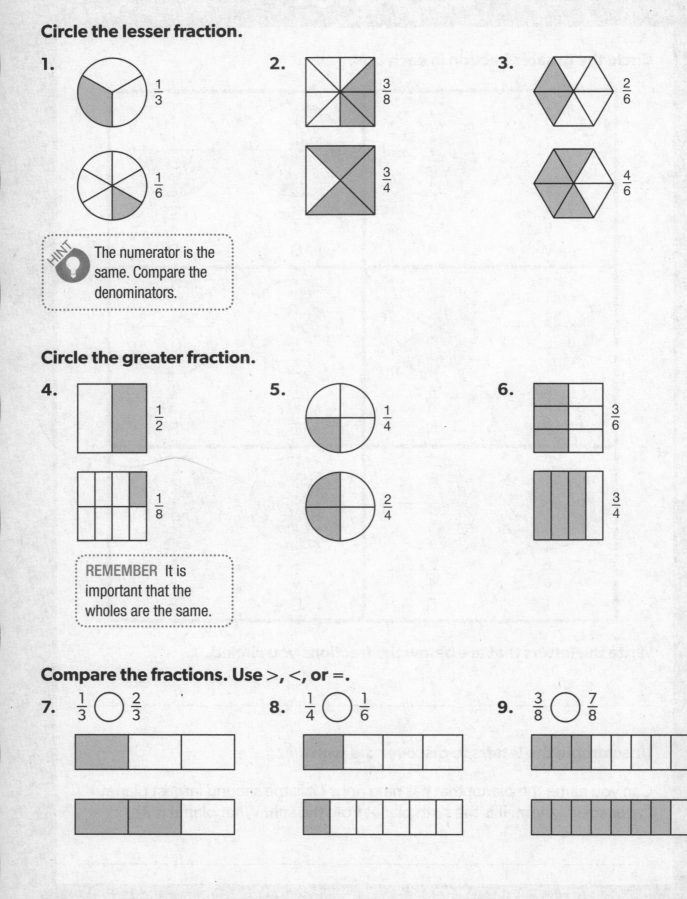

1.

$\frac{1}{3}$

$\frac{1}{6}$

2.

$\frac{3}{8}$

$\frac{3}{4}$

3.

$\frac{2}{6}$

$\frac{4}{6}$

HINT The numerator is the same. Compare the denominators.

Circle the greater fraction.

4.

$\frac{1}{2}$

$\frac{1}{8}$

5.

$\frac{1}{4}$

$\frac{2}{4}$

6.

$\frac{3}{6}$

$\frac{3}{4}$

REMEMBER It is important that the wholes are the same.

Compare the fractions. Use >, <, or =.

7. $\frac{1}{3} \bigcirc \frac{2}{3}$

8. $\frac{1}{4} \bigcirc \frac{1}{6}$

9. $\frac{3}{8} \bigcirc \frac{7}{8}$

Compare the fractions. Use >, <, or =.

10. $\frac{2}{3}$ $\bigcirc$ $\frac{2}{4}$

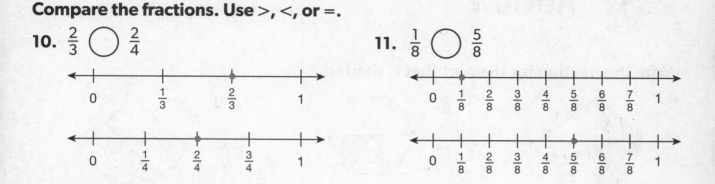

11. $\frac{1}{8}$ $\bigcirc$ $\frac{5}{8}$

Choose the best answer.

12. Which fraction is greater than $\frac{1}{3}$?

   A. $\frac{1}{6}$

   B. $\frac{1}{4}$

   C. $\frac{1}{3}$

   D. $\frac{1}{2}$

13. Which fraction is less than $\frac{3}{6}$?

   A. $\frac{1}{6}$

   B. $\frac{3}{6}$

   C. $\frac{5}{6}$

   D. $\frac{6}{6}$

Solve.

14. Ben and Rita shared a candy bar. Ben ate $\frac{1}{3}$ of the candy bar. Rita ate $\frac{1}{4}$ of the candy bar. Who ate more of the candy bar?

_____

15. Paul read $\frac{1}{6}$ of his book. Deanna read $\frac{4}{6}$ of the same book. Who read more of the book?

_____

16. **EXPLAIN** Explain why the following statement is not true. $\frac{1}{2}$ of an orange is equal to $\frac{1}{2}$ of a grape.

_____

_____

_____

17. **DRAW** Use the symbol >, <, or = to compare the fractions $\frac{2}{3}$ and $\frac{2}{8}$. Prove your answer by making a diagram.

Write the fraction for the part that is shaded.

1.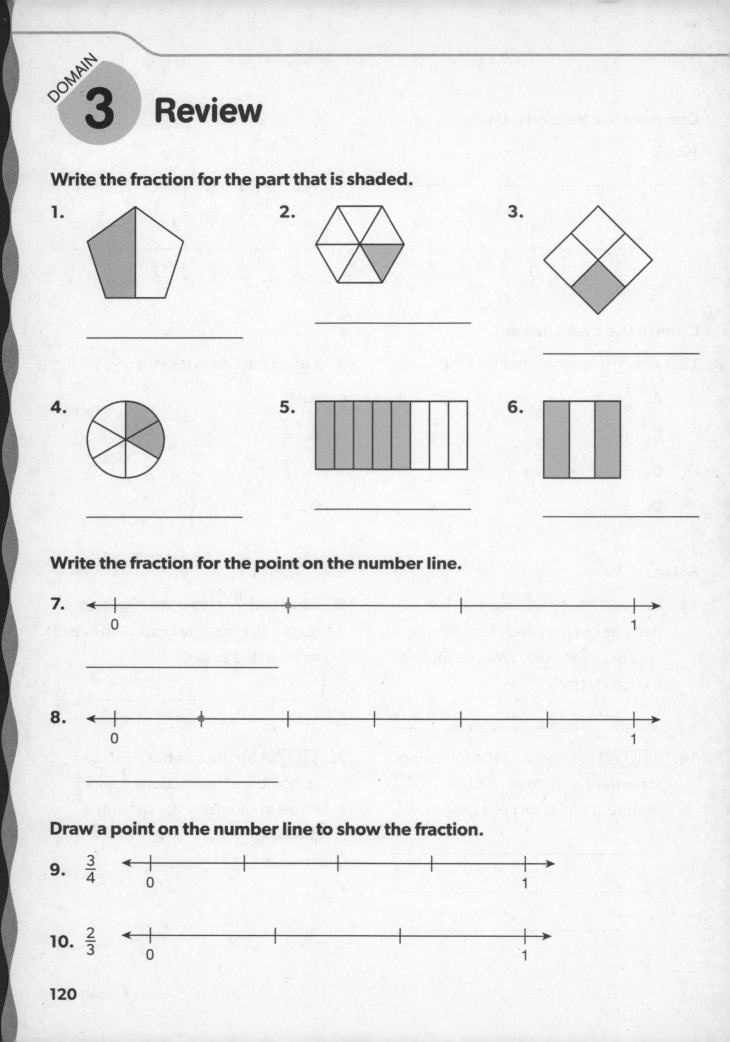

_____

2.

_____

3.

_____

4.

_____

5.

_____

6.

_____

Write the fraction for the point on the number line.

7.   0   1

_____

8.   0   1

_____

Draw a point on the number line to show the fraction.

9. $\frac{3}{4}$ 0   1

10. $\frac{2}{3}$ 0   1

Use the number lines to answer questions 11 and 12.

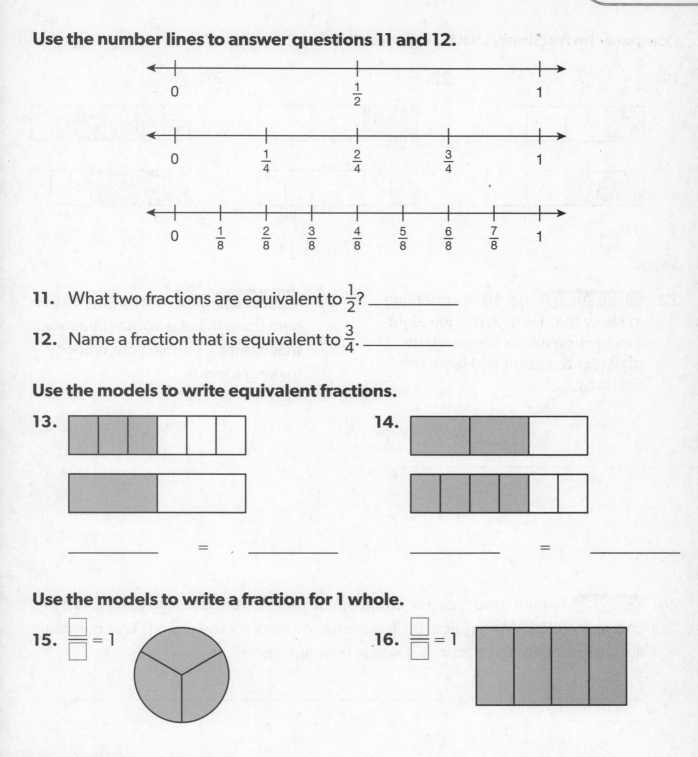

11. What two fractions are equivalent to $\frac{1}{2}$? _____

12. Name a fraction that is equivalent to $\frac{3}{4}$. _____

Use the models to write equivalent fractions.

13.

14.

_____ = _____   _____ = _____

Use the models to write a fraction for 1 whole.

15. $\frac{\square}{\square} = 1$

16. $\frac{\square}{\square} = 1$

Choose the best answer.

17. Which fraction is equivalent to 2?

A. $\frac{2}{2}$ **B.** $\frac{1}{1}$

C. $\frac{1}{2}$ **D.** $\frac{2}{1}$

18. Which fraction is equivalent to 6?

A. $\frac{3}{3}$ **B.** $\frac{6}{1}$

C. $\frac{1}{6}$ **D.** $\frac{6}{6}$

Compare the fractions. Use >, <, or =.

19. $\frac{1}{4} \bigcirc \frac{2}{4}$

20. $\frac{1}{3} \bigcirc \frac{1}{6}$

21. $\frac{5}{6} \bigcirc \frac{5}{8}$

Solve.

22. (DEMONSTRATE) Use the number line to show that 1 whole is equivalent to a fraction with a denominator of 4. Plot the point and label the fractions.

```
←——+————————————————+——→
    0                1
```

23. (ILLUSTRATE) Doug mopped $\frac{1}{3}$ of the gym floor. What is another fraction that names $\frac{1}{3}$? Show your work by making a model.

24. (COMPARE) Tamara used $\frac{2}{3}$ cup of orange juice for a recipe. She also used $\frac{2}{8}$ cup of cranberry juice. Which juice did Tamara use more of for the recipe? Use number lines to compare the fractions. Explain your answer.

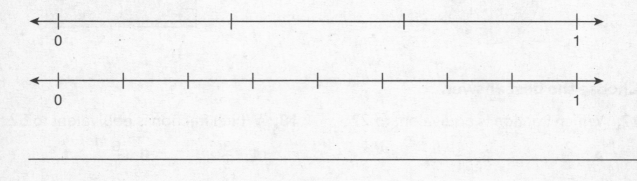

_____

_____

Four students are painting a mural. The table shows the fraction of the mural each student will paint.

Mural Painting

Name	Raul	Sumi	Ahmad	Jessica
Fraction of Mural to Paint	$\frac{1}{8}$	$\frac{3}{8}$	$\frac{1}{4}$	$\frac{2}{8}$

1. Which student paints a larger part of the mural, Raul or Jessica? Show or explain your answer.

   _____

   _____

2. Which two students paint the same fraction of the mural? Show or explain your answer.

   _____

   _____

3. Which student paints the least amount of the mural? Show or explain your answer.

   _____

   _____

4. The rectangle below is a diagram of the mural. Draw and shade the part that each student is painting. Label each part with the student's name.

Grade 2

Grade 3

Grade 4

Grade 2 MD

Measure and estimate lengths in standard units.

Relate addition and subtraction to length.

Work with time and money.

Represent and interpret data.

Grade 3 MD

Solve problems involving measurement and estimation of intervals of time, liquid volumes, and masses of objects.

Represent and interpret data.

Geometric measurement: understand concepts of area and relate area to multiplication and to addition.

Geometric measurement: recognize perimeter as an attribute of plane figures and distinguish between linear and area measures.

Grade 4 MD

Solve problems involving measurement and conversion of measurements from a larger unit to a smaller unit.

Represent and interpret data.

Grade 2 G

Reason with shapes and their attributes.

Domain 4
Measurement and Data

Time

EXAMPLE A A clock is used to tell time. What time does the clock show?

1

Look at the **hour** hand.

The hour hand is the shorter hand.

The hour hand is between 2 and 3.

It is past 2 o'clock.

2

Look at the **minute** hand.

When the minute hand moves from one number to the next, 5 minutes pass.

When the minute hand moves from one mark to the next, 1 minute passes.

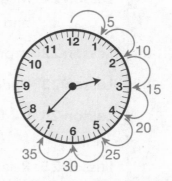

3

Tell the minutes.

The minute hand is on the second mark after the 7.

Count by 1s after 35.

35 → 36, 37

It is 37 minutes past the hour.

4

Tell the time.

The time is 37 minutes after 2 o'clock.

▶ The clock shows 2:37.

TRY

How can you write the time 2:37 in words?

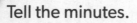

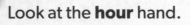

EXAMPLE B Draw hands on the clock to show that the time is 8:18.

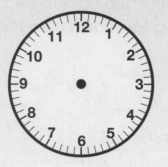

1 Find the hour.

The hour is before the colon (:).

The hour is 8 o'clock.

2 Find the minutes.

The minutes are after the colon.

The minutes are 18.

So it is 18 minutes after 8 o'clock.

3 Decide where to draw the hands.

The hour hand should point a little after 8.

When the minute hand points to the 3, it is 15 minutes after the hour.

For 18 minutes, the minute hand should point to the third mark after the 3.

4 Draw the hands on the clock.

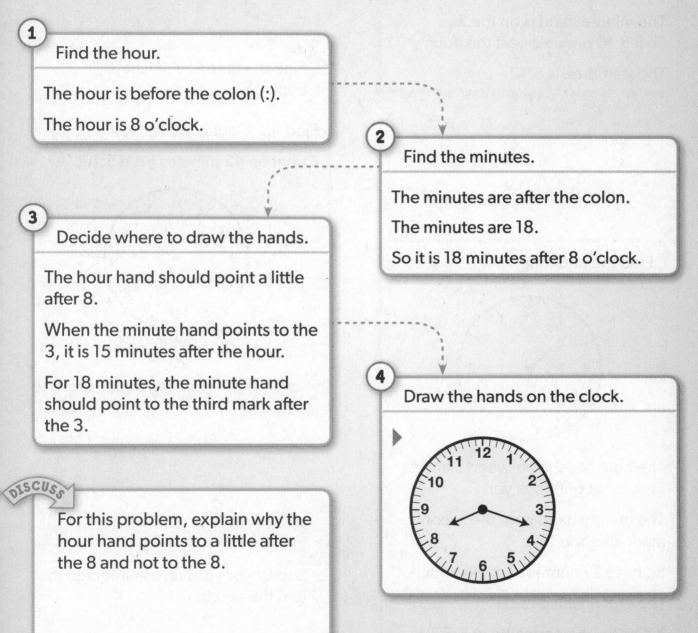

DISCUSS

For this problem, explain why the hour hand points to a little after the 8 and not to the 8.

EXAMPLE C Mia started cooking dinner at the time shown on the clock. She finished cooking 42 minutes later. What time did Mia finish cooking?

1

Find the start time.

The hour hand is between 5 and 6. So it is after 5 o'clock.

The minute hand is on the 2. So it is 10 minutes past the hour.

The start time is 5:10.

2

Find the time Mia finished cooking.

Find 42 minutes after 5:10.

Count on 42 minutes from 5:10.

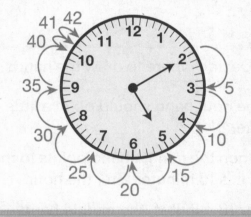

3

Find the end time.

The hour hand is between 5 and 6. So it is not 6 o'clock yet.

The minute hand is on the second mark after the 10.

So it is 52 minutes past the hour.

The end time is 5:52.

▶ Mia finished cooking at 5:52.

TRY

Show how you can use addition to find the end time.

⚙️ Problem Solving

READ

An alarm clock is a clock that makes a sound at a set time. Howard set his alarm clock for 4:45. He started taking a nap at 4:05 but did not wake up until 4:47. How long did Howard nap?

PLAN

Find how much time passed from 4:05 to 4:47.

You can subtract the times.

SOLVE

Subtract. 4:47 − 4:05

$$\begin{array}{r} 4:47 \\ -\,4:05 \\ \hline \end{array}$$

So it is _____ minutes from 4:05 to 4:47.

CHECK

Use a number line.

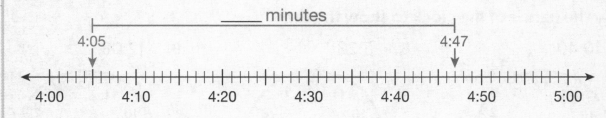

▶ Howard napped for _____ minutes.

Practice

Write the time shown on the clock.

1.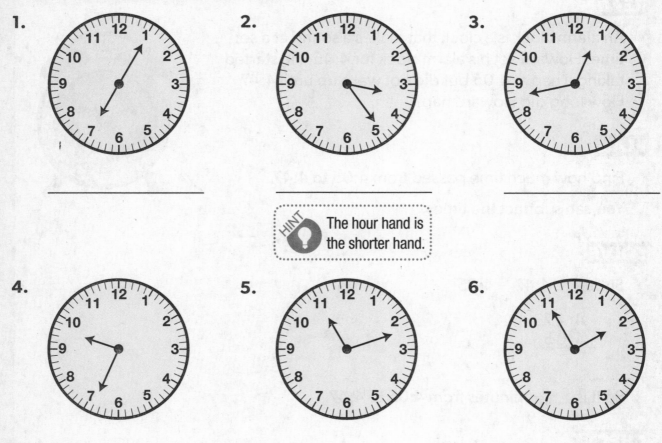

_____

2.

_____

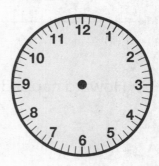 HINT The hour hand is the shorter hand.

3.

_____

4.

_____

5.

_____

6.

_____

Draw the hands of the clock to show the time.

7. 10:40

8. 5:23

9. 12:08

REMEMBER When the minute hand moves from one number to the next, 5 minutes pass.

Write how much time has passed.

10.

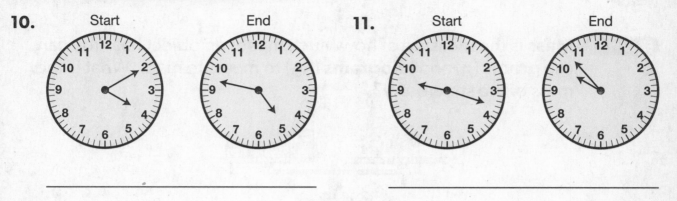

Start _____ End _____

11.

Start _____ End _____

Choose the best answer.

12. How much time passed from 1:06 to 1:28?

    A. 12 minutes

    B. 22 minutes

    C. 32 minutes

    D. 34 minutes

13. How much time passed from 8:19 to 8:58?

    A. 39 minutes

    B. 41 minutes

    C. 49 minutes

    D. 77 minutes

Solve.

14. Mary put muffins in the oven at 4:22. They need to bake for 23 minutes. What time should Mary take the muffins out of the oven?

_____

15. Carlo started reading at 8:35. He read for 18 minutes. What time did Carlos stop reading?

_____

16. **DEMONSTRATE** Deborah ate lunch from 12:15 to 12:38. How much time did Deborah spend eating lunch? Use the number line to show how to find the answer.

12:00   12:10   12:20   12:30   12:40   12:50   1:00

_____

Mass and Liquid Volume

EXAMPLE A **Mass** is the measure of how much matter an object has. You can use **grams** (**g**) and **kilograms** (**kg**) to measure mass. What is the mass of the strawberry?

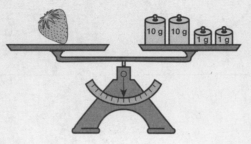

1

Use a balance scale.

The scale should be balanced.

That means the right side has the same mass as the left side.

2

Find the total mass of the weights on the right side.

There are two 10-gram weights and two 1-gram weights.

3

Find the mass of the strawberry.

Two 10-gram weights equal 20 grams.

Two 1-gram weights equal 2 grams.

20 grams + 2 grams = 22 grams

▶ The mass of the strawberry is 22 grams.

DISCUSS

Explain why it is important for the scale to be balanced.

EXAMPLE B **Liquid volume** or **capacity** is the measure of how much liquid a container can hold. You can use **milliliters** (**mL**) and **liters** (**L**) to measure liquid volume. Which is the better estimate of the liquid volume of this pot?

2 liters   2 milliliters

1 Use benchmarks.

This sports bottle holds 1 liter.

A few drops of liquid in a dropper are 1 milliliter.

1 liter

1 milliliter

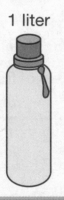

2 Compare the benchmarks with the cooking pot.

2 milliliters are a few drops of liquid.

That's too little for the cooking pot.

2 liters are about 2 sports bottles.

That's about right for the cooking pot.

▶ The cooking pot can hold about 2 liters.

DISCUSS

Explain why using benchmarks can help you estimate how much the pot can hold.

EXAMPLE C Richard bought 3 bottles of fruit punch.

How many liters of fruit punch did Richard buy in all?

1

Look at the picture.

There are 3 bottles of fruit punch.

Each bottle holds 2 liters.

2

Use multiplication to find how many liters in all.

3 × 2 liters = 6 liters

▶ Richard bought 6 liters of fruit punch in all.

CHECK

Use repeated addition to check.

2 liters + 2 liters + 2 liters = _____ liters

⚙️ Problem Solving

READ

An apple has a mass of 158 grams. A pear has a mass of 204 grams.

158 grams   204 grams

How many more grams is the pear than the apple?

PLAN

Write an equation to represent the situation.

Subtract to find how many more grams.

Let g = how many more grams

$204 - 158 = g$

SOLVE

Subtract.

$$\begin{array}{r} 204 \\ -158 \\ \hline \end{array}$$

CHECK

Use addition to check your answer.

_____ + _____ = 204

The difference, g, is _____.

➤ The pear is _____ grams more than the apple.

Practice

Circle the better unit to use to measure the mass or liquid volume.

1.

   grams
   kilograms

2.

   grams
   kilograms

3.

   milliliters
   liters

4.

   milliliters
   liters

Write how much liquid volume is in the measuring cup.

5.

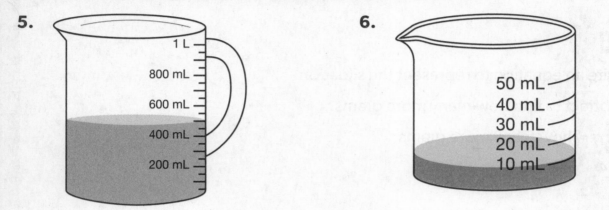

1 L

800 mL

600 mL

400 mL

200 mL

_____

6.

50 mL
40 mL
30 mL
20 mL
10 mL

_____

> **REMEMBER** Find the mark that lines up with the liquid.

Write the mass of each object.

7.

_____

8.

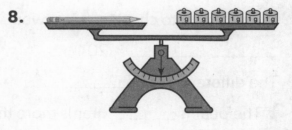

_____

Circle the better estimate of the mass.

9.

2 kilograms
20 kilograms

10.

3 grams
30 grams

11.

90 kilograms
900 kilograms

Choose the best answer.

12. About how much liquid volume can a soup spoon hold?

A. 4 milliliters   **B.** 40 milliliters

C. 4 liters   **D.** 40 liters

13. About how much liquid volume can a bathroom sink hold?

A. 1 milliliter   **B.** 10 milliliters

C. 1 liter   **D.** 10 liters

Solve.

14. A bag has 458 grams of carrots and 473 grams of celery. How many grams of vegetables are in the bag?

_____

15. The total mass of 8 quarters is 48 grams. How many grams does each quarter have?

_____

16. There are 8 jugs of orange juice on the shelf. Each jug has 3 liters. How many liters of orange juice are on the shelf in all?

_____

17. The Jones family used 228 liters of water on Monday, 196 liters on Tuesday, and 247 liters on Wednesday. How many liters of water did the Jones family use in three days?

_____

18. **EXPLAIN** Would you use grams or kilograms to measure the mass of a paperclip? Explain your answer.

_____

_____

19. **APPLY** Name 3 containers that can hold more than 1 liter of liquid volume. Explain your answer.

_____

_____

Representing Data with Picture Graphs

EXAMPLE A A **picture graph** uses symbols to represent **data**. The picture graph below shows the miles that some students rode their bikes.

Miles Traveled by Bike

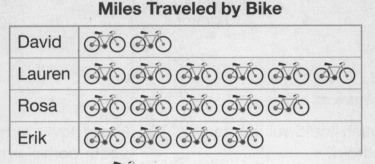

Key: Each 🚲 = 2 miles

How many miles did Rosa ride her bike?

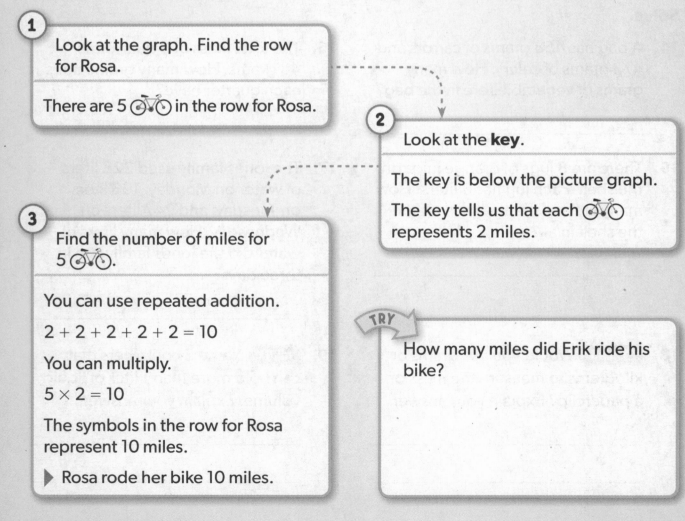

1

Look at the graph. Find the row for Rosa.

There are 5 🚲 in the row for Rosa.

2

Look at the **key**.

The key is below the picture graph.

The key tells us that each 🚲 represents 2 miles.

3

Find the number of miles for 5 🚲.

You can use repeated addition.

2 + 2 + 2 + 2 + 2 = 10

You can multiply.

5 × 2 = 10

The symbols in the row for Rosa represent 10 miles.

▶ Rosa rode her bike 10 miles.

TRY

How many miles did Erik ride his bike?

EXAMPLE B The picture graph below shows the number of runs scored by some baseball teams.

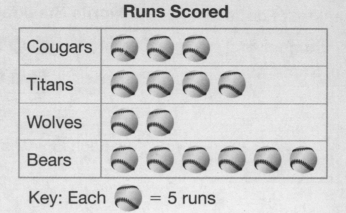

Runs Scored

Key: Each 🏐 = 5 runs

Which team scored the greatest number of runs? How many runs did that team score?

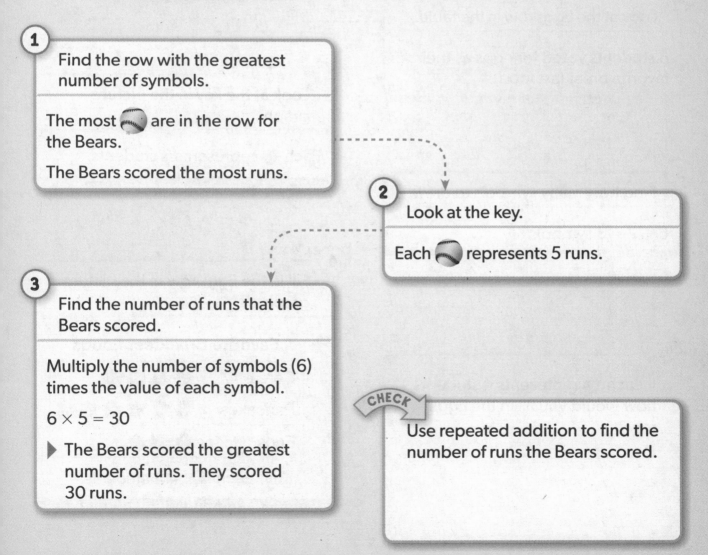

1

Find the row with the greatest number of symbols.

The most 🏐 are in the row for the Bears.

The Bears scored the most runs.

2

Look at the key.

Each 🏐 represents 5 runs.

3

Find the number of runs that the Bears scored.

Multiply the number of symbols (6) times the value of each symbol.

$6 \times 5 = 30$

▶ The Bears scored the greatest number of runs. They scored 30 runs.

CHECK

Use repeated addition to find the number of runs the Bears scored.

EXAMPLE C The table and picture graph show some students' favorite breakfast foods.

Favorite Breakfast Foods

Food	Number of Students
Cereal	8
Pancakes	12
Eggs	6

Favorite Breakfast Foods

Cereal	✹✹✹✹
Pancakes	✹✹✹✹✹✹
Eggs	

Key: Each ✹ = 2 students

Fill in the Eggs row in the picture graph.

1 Look at the Eggs row in the table.

6 students voted for eggs as their favorite breakfast food.

2 Look at the key in the picture graph.

Each ✹ represents 2 students.

3 Find how many symbols to draw.

6 ÷ 2 = 3 symbols

4 Fill in the Eggs row in the picture graph.

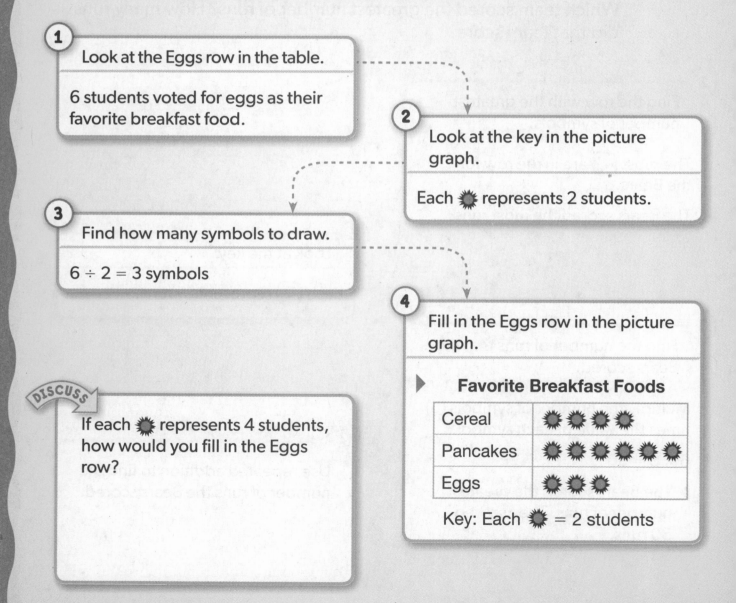

Favorite Breakfast Foods

Cereal	✹✹✹✹
Pancakes	✹✹✹✹✹
Eggs	✹✹✹

Key: Each ✹ = 2 students

DISCUSS

If each ✹ represents 4 students, how would you fill in the Eggs row?

EXAMPLE D The table and picture graph show information about Hanna's lemonade sales.

Hanna's Lemonade Sales

Day	Number of Glasses
Thursday	15
Friday	25
Saturday	20
Sunday	10

Hanna's Lemonade Sales

Thursday	
Friday	
Saturday	
Sunday	

Key: Each 🥤 = 5 glasses sold

Complete the picture graph to match the data in the table.

1

Look at the key in the picture graph.

Each 🥤 represents 5 glasses sold.

2

Find how many symbols to draw for each day.

Thursday: 15 ÷ 5 = 3 symbols

Friday: 25 ÷ 5 = 5 symbols

Saturday: 20 ÷ 5 = 4 symbols

Sunday: 10 ÷ 5 = 2 symbols

3

Fill in the picture graph.

▶ **Hanna's Lemonade Sales**

Thursday	🥤🥤🥤
Friday	🥤🥤🥤🥤🥤
Saturday	🥤🥤🥤🥤
Sunday	🥤🥤

Key: Each 🥤 = 5 glasses sold

TRY

If each 🥤 represents 10 glasses, how many 🥤 would you need to draw for Saturday?

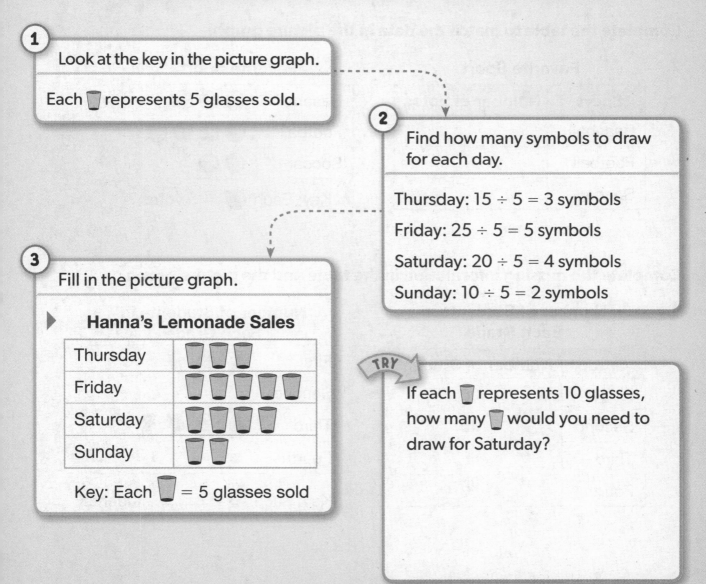

Practice

Complete the picture graph to match the data in the table.

1. **Number of Books Read**

Student	Number of Books
Max	8
Ling	10
Katie	6

Number of Books Read

Max	
Ling	
Katie	

Key: Each 📖 = 2 books

> REMEMBER Use the key to decide how many symbols to draw.

Complete the table to match the data in the picture graph.

2. **Favorite Sport**

Sport	Number of Votes
Baseball	
Football	
Soccer	

Favorite Sport

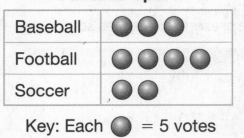

Key: Each ⬤ = 5 votes

Complete the missing information in the table and the picture graph.

3. **Number of Students in Each Grade**

Grade	Number of Students
First	30
Second	40
Third	
Fourth	50

Number of Students in Each Grade

First	🧍🧍🧍
Second	
Third	🧍🧍🧍🧍
Fourth	

Key: Each 🧍 = _____ students

Choose the best answer.

4. In a picture graph, 6 🚗 represent 30 cars. Which could be the key of the picture graph?

    A. Each 🚗 = 1 car

    B. Each 🚗 = 2 cars

    C. Each 🚗 = 5 cars

    D. Each 🚗 = 10 cars

5. In a picture graph, 10 ⬤ represent 20 points. Which could be the key of the picture graph?

    A. Each ⬤ = 1 point

    B. Each ⬤ = 2 points

    C. Each ⬤ = 5 points

    D. Each ⬤ = 10 points

Use the picture graph for questions 6–9.

Recycling Drive

Patsy	🗑️🗑️🗑️🗑️
Juan	🗑️🗑️🗑️🗑️🗑️
Tai	🗑️🗑️🗑️
Ellen	🗑️🗑️🗑️🗑️

Key: Each 🗑️ = 10 cans

6. Who collected the greatest number of cans? How many cans did that person collect?

    _____

7. If each symbol represented 5 cans, how many symbols would be needed for Juan's row?

    _____

8. How many cans did the 4 people collect in all? Show how you found your answer.

    _____

    _____

9. **EXPLAIN** Why do you need a key for a picture graph? Explain your answer.

    _____

    _____

EXAMPLE A A **bar graph** uses bars of different lengths to represent data. The bar graph below shows the number of tickets some students sold.

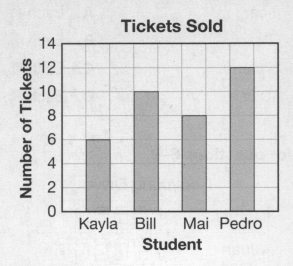

How many tickets did Bill sell?

1

Look at the graph. Find the column for Bill.

There are 5 squares shaded in the column for Bill.

2

Look at the **scale**.

The scale is on the left side of the bar graph.

This bar graph has a scale of 2. So, each square equals 2 tickets sold.

3

Find the number of tickets Bill sold.

Look at the top of the column for Bill.

Read the number on the scale that lines up with the top of the column.

▶ Bill sold 10 tickets.

TRY

How many tickets did Mai sell?

EXAMPLE B The bar graph below shows the pets owned by the children in the Roosevelt School.

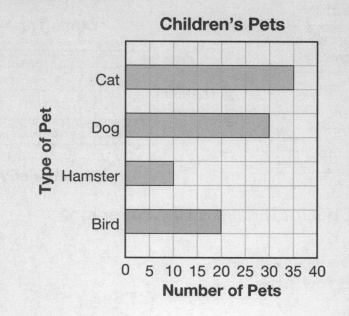

Children's Pets

Type of Pet: Cat, Dog, Hamster, Bird
Number of Pets: 0 5 10 15 20 25 30 35 40

How many children have a dog as a pet?

1 Look at the graph. Find the row for Dog.

The row for Dog has 6 squares shaded.

2 Look at the scale.

The scale is at the bottom of the bar graph.

This bar graph has a scale of 5. So, each square equals 5 pets.

3 Find the number of children who have a dog as a pet.

Look at the end of the bar for Dog. The end is the side farthest from 0.

Read the number on the scale that lines up with the end of the bar.

▶ 30 children have a dog as a pet.

TRY
How many children in all have dogs and cats as pets?

EXAMPLE C The table and bar graph show students' class trip votes.

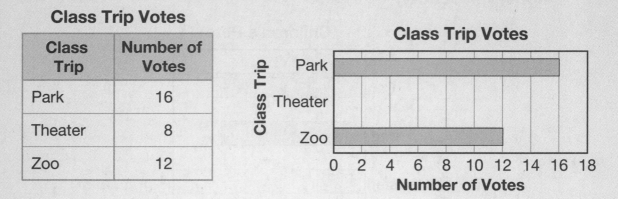

Class Trip Votes

Class Trip	Number of Votes
Park	16
Theater	8
Zoo	12

Class Trip Votes

Draw the bar for Theater on the bar graph.

1 Look at the Theater row in the table.

8 students voted for the theater for their class trip.

2 Look at the scale on the bar graph.

The scale of this graph is 2.

3 Fill in the Theater bar on the bar graph.

Shade the bar up to 8.

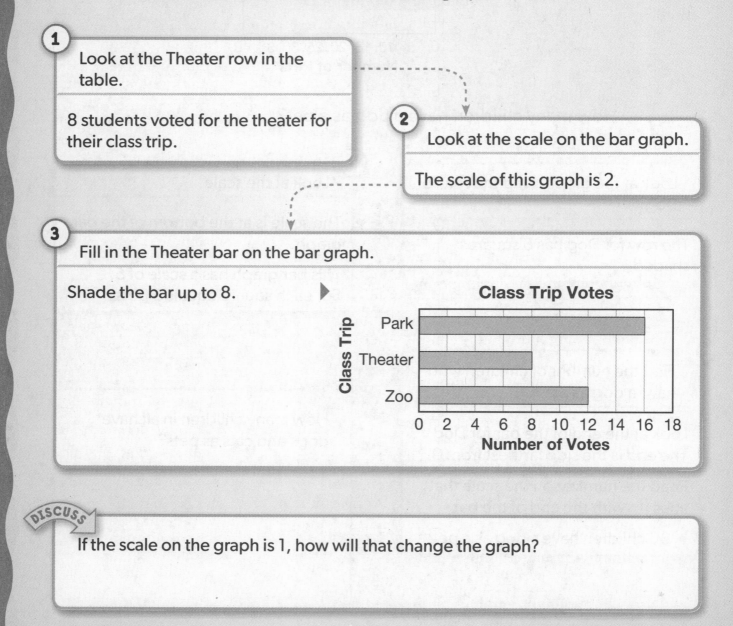

Class Trip Votes

DISCUSS

If the scale on the graph is 1, how will that change the graph?

EXAMPLE D The table and bar graph show the flowers Emily has in her garden.

Flowers in Emily's Garden

Type of Flower	Number of Flowers
Rose	15
Tulip	35
Daisy	10
Lily	25

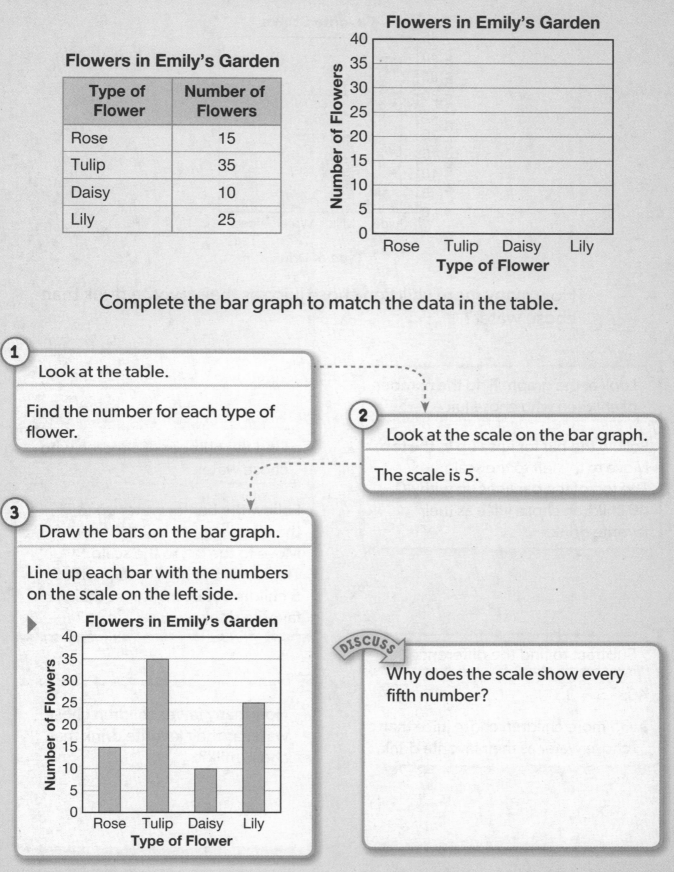

Flowers in Emily's Garden

Complete the bar graph to match the data in the table.

1 Look at the table.

Find the number for each type of flower.

2 Look at the scale on the bar graph.

The scale is 5.

3 Draw the bars on the bar graph.

Line up each bar with the numbers on the scale on the left side.

Flowers in Emily's Garden

DISCUSS Why does the scale show every fifth number?

EXAMPLE E The bar graph shows the favorite drinks of some children.

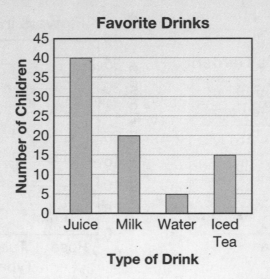

How many more children chose juice as their favorite drink than chose water?

1

Look at the graph. Find the number of children who chose juice.

Follow the bar for juice up to the top.
Move to the left to the scale.
The top of the bar lines up with 40.
40 children chose juice as their favorite drink.

2

Find the number of children who chose water.

Follow the bar for water up to the top.
Move to the left to the scale.
The top of the bar lines up with 5.
5 children chose water as their favorite drink.

3

Subtract to find the difference.

40 − 5 = 35

▶ 35 more children chose juice than chose water as their favorite drink.

TRY

How many fewer children chose water as their favorite drink than chose milk?

⚙ Problem Solving

READ

The bar graph shows the stamps in Melanie's stamp collection.

How many fewer stamps from the United States does Melanie have than stamps from Mexico and China combined?

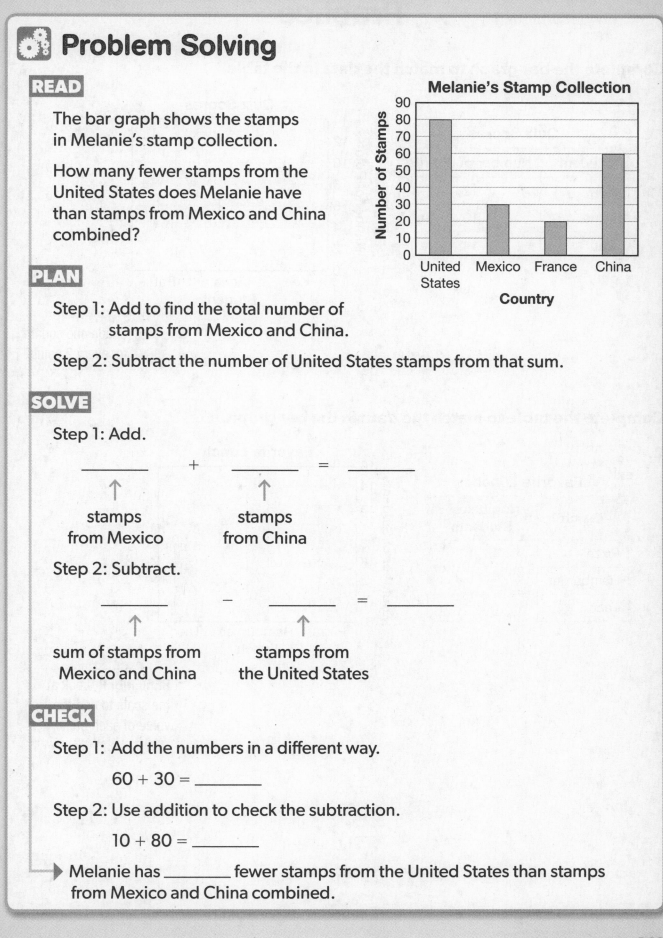

Melanie's Stamp Collection

PLAN

Step 1: Add to find the total number of stamps from Mexico and China.

Step 2: Subtract the number of United States stamps from that sum.

SOLVE

Step 1: Add.

_____ + _____ = _____

↑   ↑

stamps   stamps
from Mexico   from China

Step 2: Subtract.

_____ – _____ = _____

↑   ↑

sum of stamps from   stamps from
Mexico and China   the United States

CHECK

Step 1: Add the numbers in a different way.

60 + 30 = _____

Step 2: Use addition to check the subtraction.

10 + 80 = _____

▶ Melanie has _____ fewer stamps from the United States than stamps from Mexico and China combined.

Practice

Complete the bar graph to match the data in the table.

1.

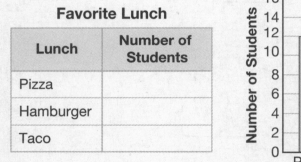

Quiz Scores

Student	Number of Points
Ken	12
Anna	10
Pat	14

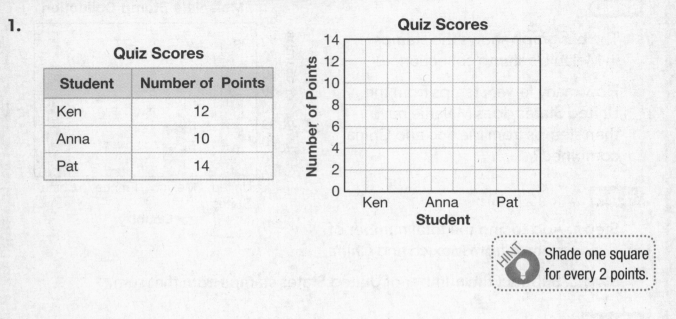

> HINT Shade one square for every 2 points.

Complete the table to match the data in the bar graph.

2.

Favorite Lunch

Lunch	Number of Students
Pizza	
Hamburger	
Taco	

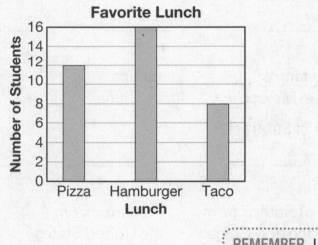

> REMEMBER Look at the scale to find the value of each bar.

Use the bar graph for questions 3 and 4.

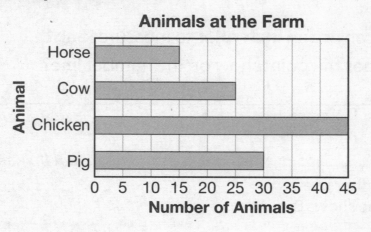

3. How many fewer pigs than chickens are at the farm?

_____

4. How many more chickens than cows and horses combined does the farm have?

_____

Use the bar graph for questions 5–7.

5. How many more customers did the store have on Sunday than on Saturday?

_____

6. How many fewer customers visited the store on Thursday than on Friday?

_____

7. **CREATE** Use the data in the graph to create a word problem. Give the problem to a classmate to solve.

_____

_____

Measuring Length to the Nearest $\frac{1}{2}$ Inch and $\frac{1}{4}$ Inch

UNDERSTAND You can use an **inch ruler** to measure **length**.

What number does the point show on the number line?

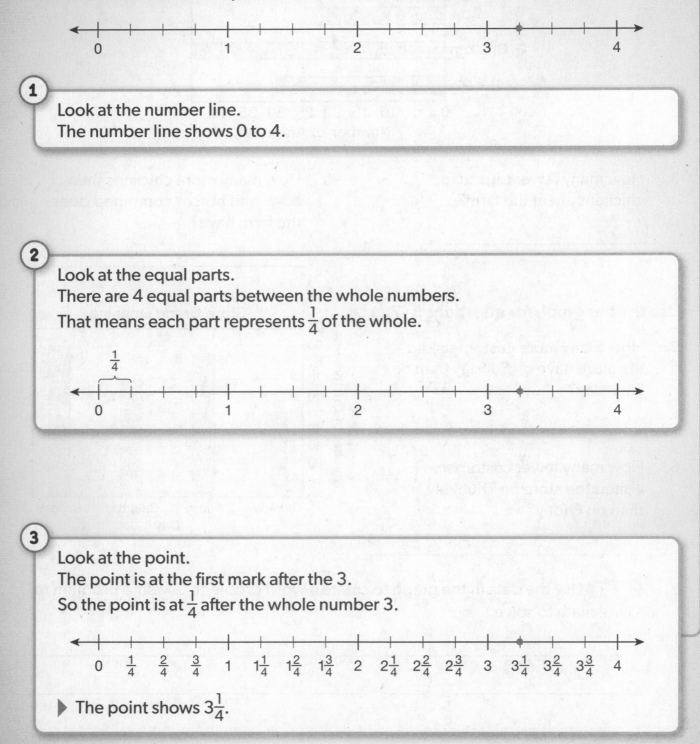

1

Look at the number line.
The number line shows 0 to 4.

2

Look at the equal parts.
There are 4 equal parts between the whole numbers.
That means each part represents $\frac{1}{4}$ of the whole.

3

Look at the point.
The point is at the first mark after the 3.
So the point is at $\frac{1}{4}$ after the whole number 3.

▶ The point shows $3\frac{1}{4}$.

⊸⊏ Connect

What is the length of this crayon to the nearest $\frac{1}{4}$ **inch**?

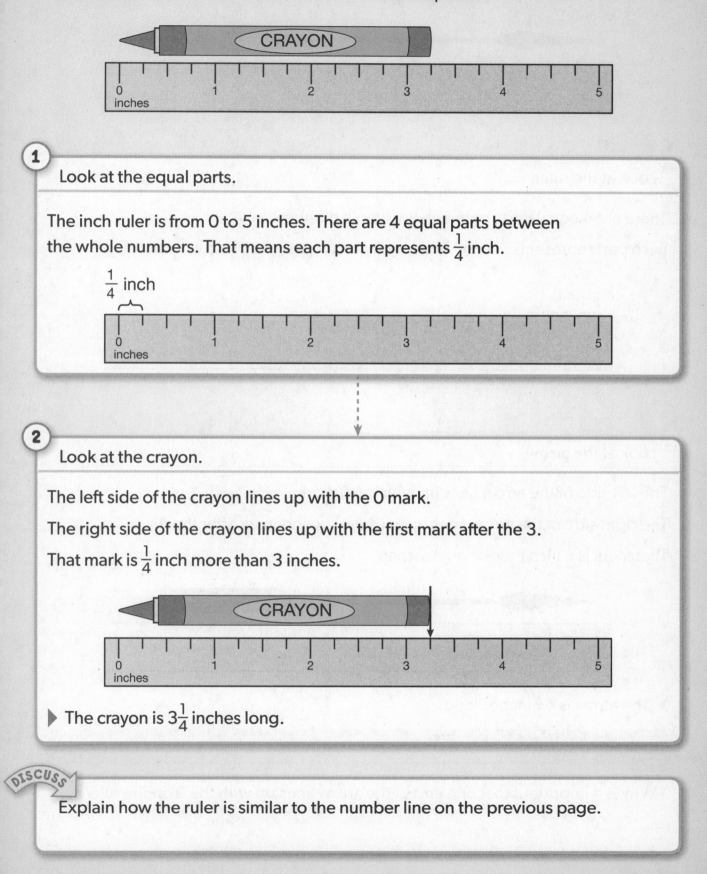

1

Look at the equal parts.

The inch ruler is from 0 to 5 inches. There are 4 equal parts between the whole numbers. That means each part represents $\frac{1}{4}$ inch.

2

Look at the crayon.

The left side of the crayon lines up with the 0 mark.

The right side of the crayon lines up with the first mark after the 3.

That mark is $\frac{1}{4}$ inch more than 3 inches.

▶ The crayon is $3\frac{1}{4}$ inches long.

DISCUSS

Explain how the ruler is similar to the number line on the previous page.

EXAMPLE A What is the length of this arrow to the nearest $\frac{1}{2}$ inch?

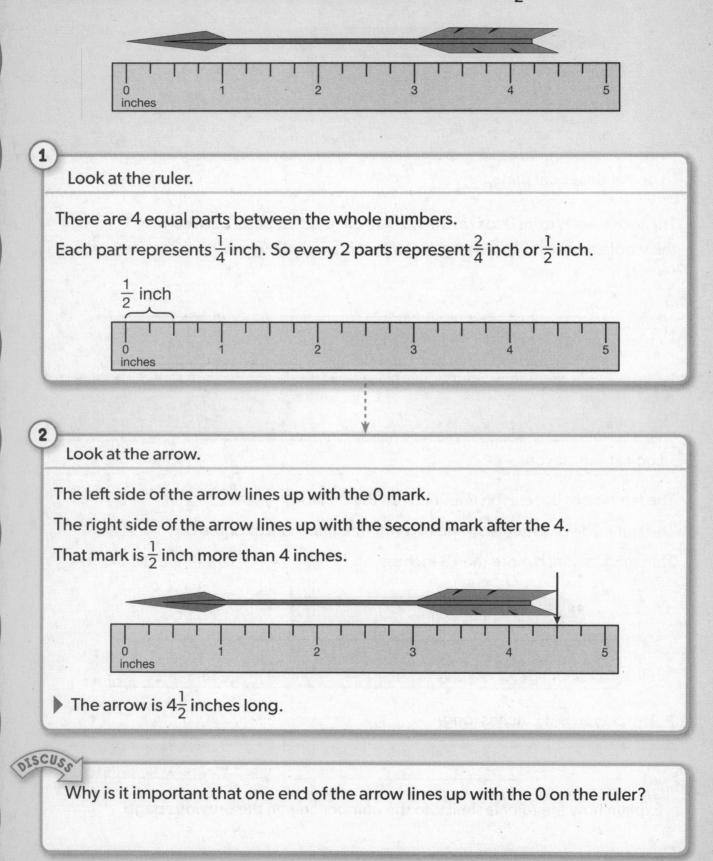

1

Look at the ruler.

There are 4 equal parts between the whole numbers.

Each part represents $\frac{1}{4}$ inch. So every 2 parts represent $\frac{2}{4}$ inch or $\frac{1}{2}$ inch.

2

Look at the arrow.

The left side of the arrow lines up with the 0 mark.

The right side of the arrow lines up with the second mark after the 4.

That mark is $\frac{1}{2}$ inch more than 4 inches.

▶ The arrow is $4\frac{1}{2}$ inches long.

DISCUSS

Why is it important that one end of the arrow lines up with the 0 on the ruler?

EXAMPLE B Kerri has a bracelet that is $3\frac{3}{4}$ inches long.

Draw a $3\frac{3}{4}$-inch line to represent Kerri's bracelet.

1 Use an inch ruler. Look at the marks on the ruler.

Each mark on the ruler is $\frac{1}{4}$ inch.

Look for the $3\frac{3}{4}$-inch mark on the ruler.

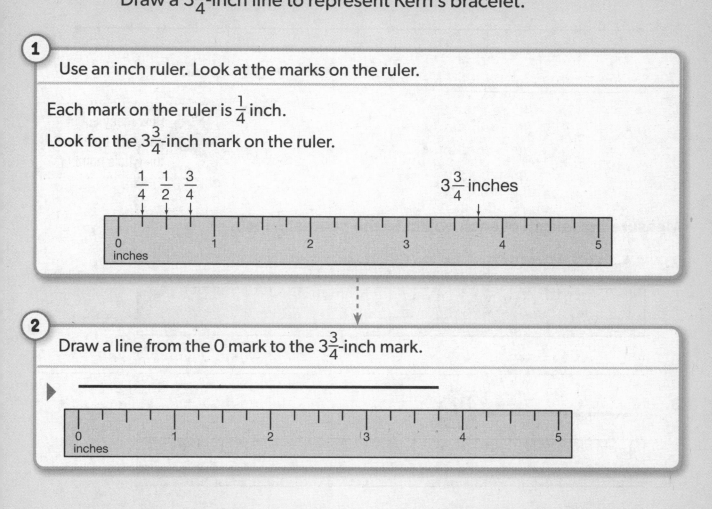

2 Draw a line from the 0 mark to the $3\frac{3}{4}$-inch mark.

TRY Draw a line that is $2\frac{2}{4}$ inches long.

Practice

What number does the point show on the number line?

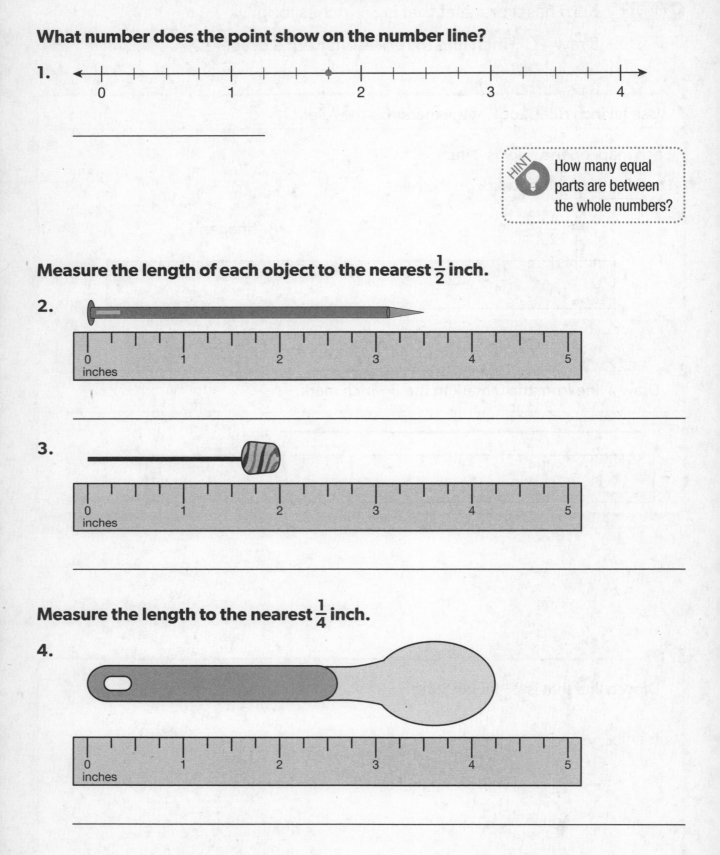

1.

_____

HINT How many equal parts are between the whole numbers?

Measure the length of each object to the nearest $\frac{1}{2}$ inch.

2.

_____

3.

_____

Measure the length to the nearest $\frac{1}{4}$ inch.

4.

_____

Use a ruler to measure the length of each object to the nearest $\frac{1}{4}$ inch.

5.

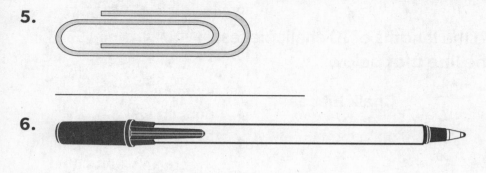

_____

6.

_____

Choose the best answer.

7. To the nearest $\frac{1}{4}$ inch, which is closest to the length of this toothbrush?

    A. 4 inches

    B. $4\frac{1}{2}$ inches

    C. $4\frac{3}{4}$ inches

    D. 5 inches

Use an inch ruler to draw a line of the given length.

8. $1\frac{1}{2}$ inches

9. $2\frac{3}{4}$ inches

Solve.

10. **DESCRIBE** Explain how you can use an inch ruler to measure the length of an object.

_____

_____

_____

LESSON 22 Representing Data with Line Plots

EXAMPLE A Jill measured the lengths of 10 chalk pieces. She made the **line plot** below.

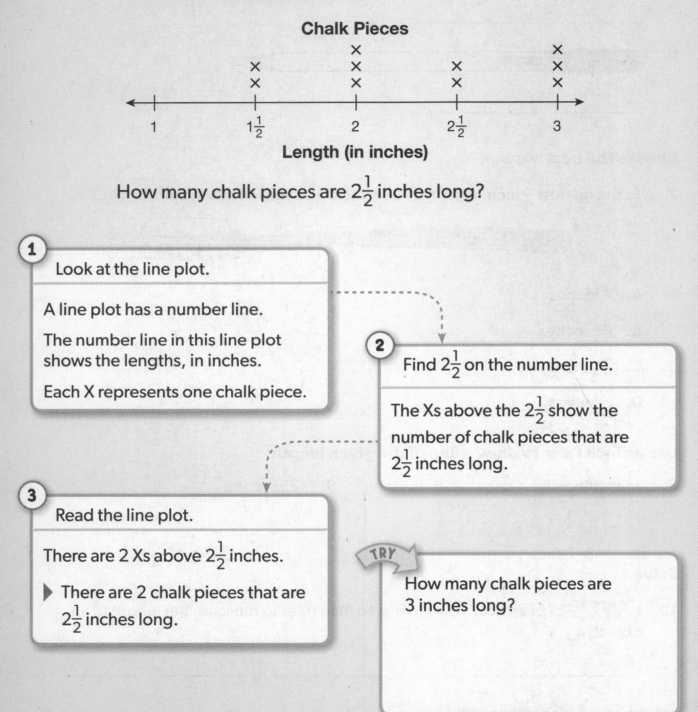

How many chalk pieces are $2\frac{1}{2}$ inches long?

1

Look at the line plot.

A line plot has a number line.

The number line in this line plot shows the lengths, in inches.

Each X represents one chalk piece.

2

Find $2\frac{1}{2}$ on the number line.

The Xs above the $2\frac{1}{2}$ show the number of chalk pieces that are $2\frac{1}{2}$ inches long.

3

Read the line plot.

There are 2 Xs above $2\frac{1}{2}$ inches.

▶ There are 2 chalk pieces that are $2\frac{1}{2}$ inches long.

TRY

How many chalk pieces are 3 inches long?

EXAMPLE B Frank measured 12 ribbons. He listed the lengths in the table below.

Ribbon Lengths

Length (in inches)	5	$5\frac{1}{4}$	$5\frac{2}{4}$	$5\frac{3}{4}$	6	$6\frac{1}{4}$	$6\frac{2}{4}$
Number of Ribbons	1	3	0	4	1	2	1

Make a line plot to show the lengths of the ribbons.

1

Start the line plot.

Start with a number line. Make the number line from 5 to $6\frac{2}{4}$ inches.

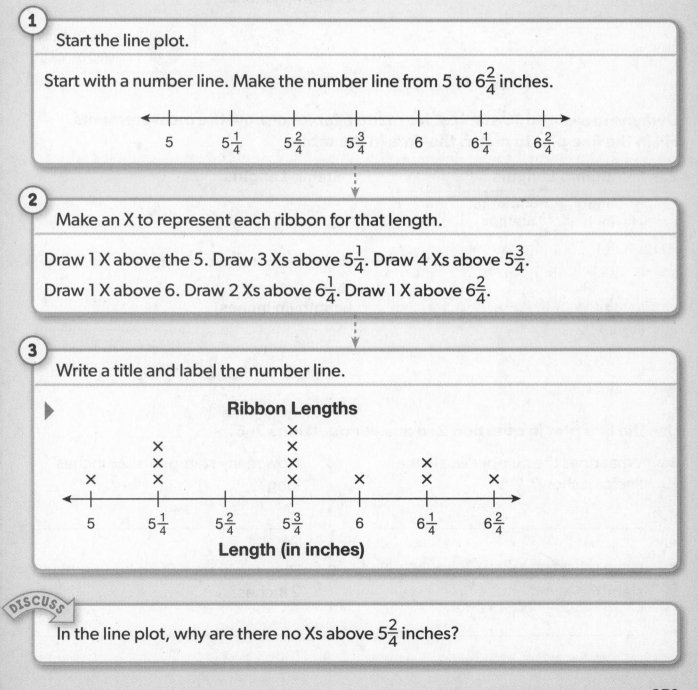

2

Make an X to represent each ribbon for that length.

Draw 1 X above the 5. Draw 3 Xs above $5\frac{1}{4}$. Draw 4 Xs above $5\frac{3}{4}$.

Draw 1 X above 6. Draw 2 Xs above $6\frac{1}{4}$. Draw 1 X above $6\frac{2}{4}$.

3

Write a title and label the number line.

Ribbon Lengths

Length (in inches)

DISCUSS

In the line plot, why are there no Xs above $5\frac{2}{4}$ inches?

Practice

Trina measured 12 colored pencils. She made a table and started a line plot. Finish the line plot for Trina.

1. **Colored Pencil Lengths**

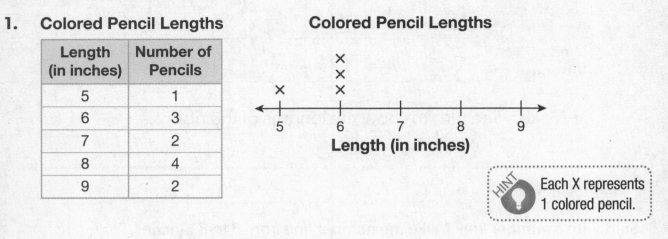

Length (in inches)	Number of Pencils
5	1
6	3
7	2
8	4
9	2

Colored Pencil Lengths

Length (in inches)

HINT Each X represents 1 colored pencil.

Dwayne measured 10 stamps. He made a table to show the measurements. Fill in the line plot to match the data in the table.

2. **Stamp Lengths**

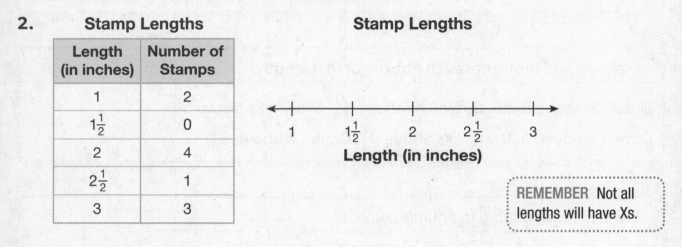

Length (in inches)	Number of Stamps
1	2
$1\frac{1}{2}$	0
2	4
$2\frac{1}{2}$	1
3	3

Stamp Lengths

Length (in inches)

REMEMBER Not all lengths will have Xs.

Use the line plot in question 2 to answer questions 3–6.

3. What does the number line in the line plot show?

_____

4. How many stamps are $2\frac{1}{2}$ inches long?

_____

5. What is the length of the shortest stamp?

_____

6. How many stamps are longer than 2 inches?

_____

Izra measured some nails. He made a line plot to show the measurements. Fill in the table to match the data in the line plot.

7.

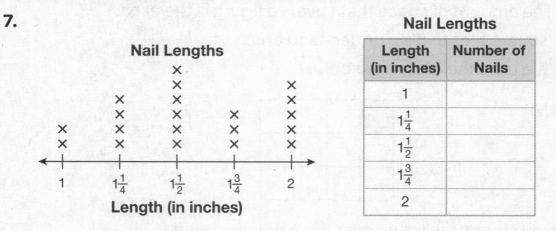

Nail Lengths

Length (in inches)	Number of Nails
1	
$1\frac{1}{4}$	
$1\frac{1}{2}$	
$1\frac{3}{4}$	
2	

Use the line plot in question 7 to answer questions 8–12.

8. How many nails are $1\frac{1}{4}$ inches long?

_____

9. How many nails are longer than $1\frac{1}{2}$ inches?

_____

10. How many more $1\frac{1}{2}$-inch nails are there than 1-inch nails?

_____

11. How many nails did Izra measure?

_____

Shannon measured some stickers in her sticker book. She made the table below. Use the data to make a line plot in the box.

12. DEMONSTRATE

Sticker Lengths

Length (in inches)	Number of Stickers
$\frac{1}{2}$	3
$\frac{3}{4}$	2
1	6
$1\frac{1}{4}$	4
$1\frac{1}{2}$	2

LESSON 23 Understanding Area

UNDERSTAND The amount of space that covers a figure is the **area**.

You can use square tiles to help understand area.

One square tile is on the **rectangle** below.

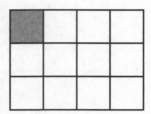

Find how many square tiles can cover the whole rectangle.

1

The square tile has a side length of 1 unit.

= 1 square unit

So the whole tile is 1 unit square.

2

Use square tiles to fill the whole rectangle.
There should be no gaps between the tiles.
The tiles should not overlap.

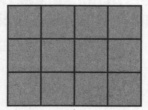

So the tiles show the area of the rectangle.

3

Count how many square tiles cover the whole rectangle.

▶ 12 square tiles cover the rectangle.

◂⊏ Connect

Each square in the grid below has an area of 1 square unit.

Draw a rectangle with an area of 12 square units on the grid.

1

Look at the squares in the grid.

☐ = 1 square unit

Each square has a side length of 1 unit.

So each square is 1 unit square.

It has an area of 1 **square unit**.

2

Draw a rectangle with an area of 12 square units.

Count 12 unit squares to make a rectangle.

Shade the squares.

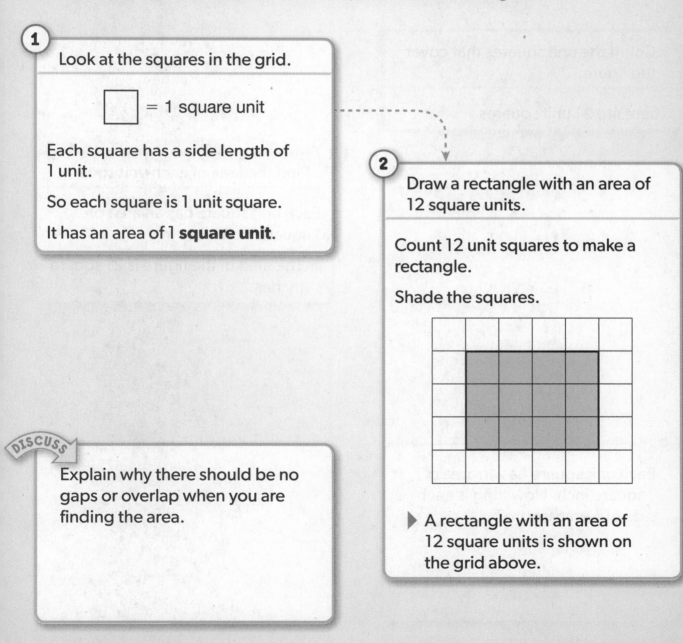

▶ A rectangle with an area of 12 square units is shown on the grid above.

DISCUSS

Explain why there should be no gaps or overlap when you are finding the area.

EXAMPLE A What is the area of this figure?

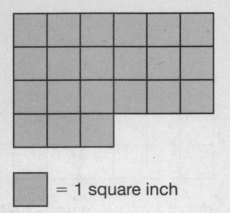

= 1 square inch

1

Count the unit squares that cover the figure.

There are 21 unit squares.

2

Find the area of each unit square.

Each unit square has an area of 1 square inch.

▶ The area of the figure is 21 square inches.

DISCUSS

Each unit square has an area of 1 square inch. How long is each side of a unit square?

EXAMPLE B The floor of a bedroom closet is in the shape of a rectangle. It has an area of 18 square feet. Draw a diagram in the grid below to show the floor.

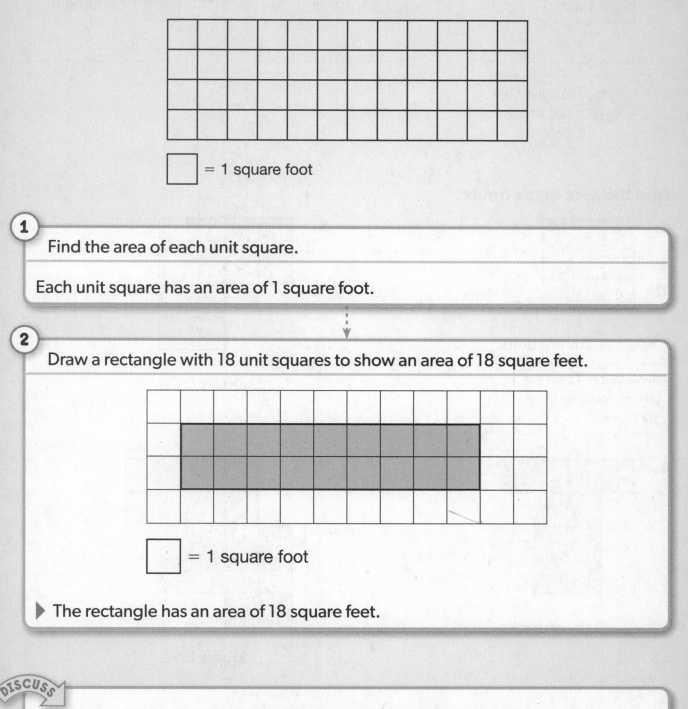

☐ = 1 square foot

1

Find the area of each unit square.

Each unit square has an area of 1 square foot.

2

Draw a rectangle with 18 unit squares to show an area of 18 square feet.

☐ = 1 square foot

▶ The rectangle has an area of 18 square feet.

DISCUSS

If the closet has an area of 9 square feet, how does that change the diagram above?

Practice

What is the area of the square?

1. ☐ 1 inch

_____

2. ☐ 1 meter

_____

3. ☐ 1 centimeter

_____

> **HINT** 💡 This square has a side length of 1 inch.

Find the area of the figure.

4.

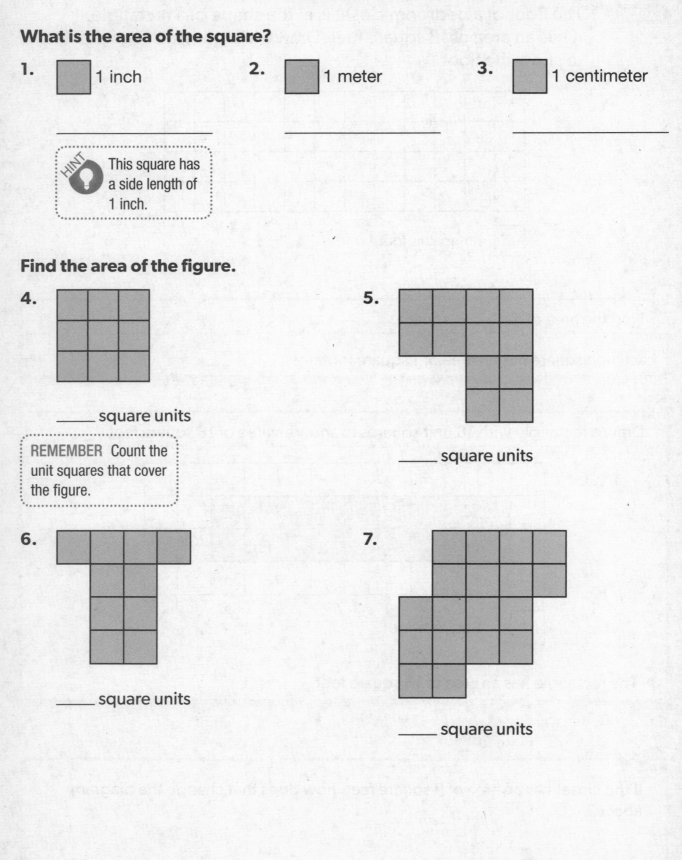

_____ square units

> **REMEMBER** Count the unit squares that cover the figure.

5.

_____ square units

6.

_____ square units

7.

_____ square units

Draw a figure with the given area on the grid.

8. 15 square units

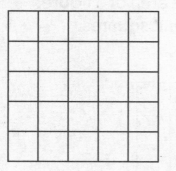

9. 22 square units

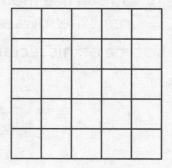

Choose the best answer.

10. What is the area of the figure?

= 1 square meter

A. 18 meters

B. 18 square meters

C. 18 square inches

D. 18 square feet

11. What is the area of the figure?

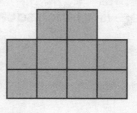

= 1 square inch

A. 12 inches

B. 12 square inches

C. 10 inches

D. 10 square inches

Solve.

12. **ILLUSTRATE** Draw 3 different figures with an area of 14 square units on the grid below.

= 1 square unit

Using Multiplication to Solve Area Problems

UNDERSTAND You can use multiplication to find the area of a figure. Count the rows and columns of the unit squares.

What is the area of this rectangle?

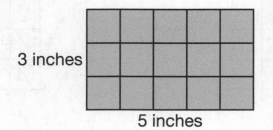

3 inches

5 inches

1

Each square is a 1-inch square.

□ = 1 square inch

2

Count the rows and columns of the rectangle.
There are 3 rows of inch squares.
There are 5 columns of inch squares.

3

Find the total.
3 rows of 5 equal 15.
There are 15 inch squares.

▶ The rectangle has an area of 15 square inches.

◄ Connect

What is the area of this rectangle?

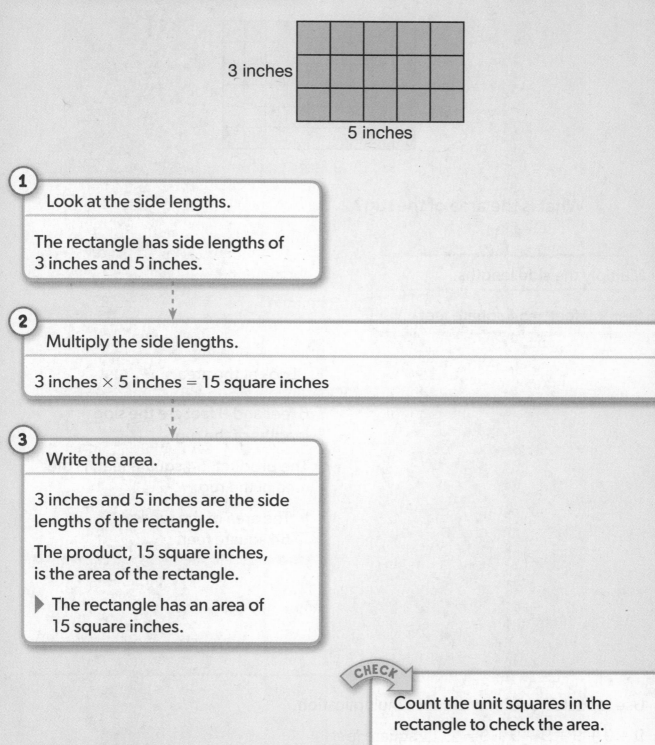

3 inches

5 inches

1 Look at the side lengths.

The rectangle has side lengths of 3 inches and 5 inches.

2 Multiply the side lengths.

3 inches × 5 inches = 15 square inches

3 Write the area.

3 inches and 5 inches are the side lengths of the rectangle.

The product, 15 square inches, is the area of the rectangle.

▶ The rectangle has an area of 15 square inches.

CHECK

Count the unit squares in the rectangle to check the area.

EXAMPLE Nicole drew a diagram of the rug in the classroom.

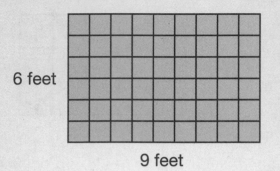

6 feet

9 feet

What is the area of the rug?

1 Multiply the side lengths.

6 feet × 9 feet = 54 square feet

2 Look at the area.

6 feet and 9 feet are the side lengths of the rug.

The product, 54 square feet, is the area of the rug.

▶ The area of the rug is 54 square feet.

CHECK

Use repeated addition to check multiplication.

9 + 9 + 9 + 9 + 9 + 9 = _____ square feet

⚙ Problem Solving

READ

A garden has an area of 40 square meters.

One of the side lengths is 8 meters.

What is the missing side length of the garden?

? meters

8 meters

PLAN

Write an equation to represent the area.

You know one of the side lengths and the area.

Let s = the missing side length

$8 \times s = 40$

SOLVE

Find the missing factor, s.

Use a related division fact.

$40 \div 8 = \underline{\hspace{1cm}}$

So $8 \times \underline{\hspace{1cm}} = 40$.

$s = \underline{\hspace{1cm}}$

CHECK

Use repeated addition.

Add 8 five times.

$\underline{\hspace{1cm}} + \underline{\hspace{1cm}} + \underline{\hspace{1cm}} + \underline{\hspace{1cm}} + \underline{\hspace{1cm}} = 40$

The missing factor, s, is \underline{\hspace{2cm}}.

So the other side length is \underline{\hspace{2cm}} meters.

▶ The missing side length is \underline{\hspace{2cm}} meters.

Practice

Find the area of the rectangle.

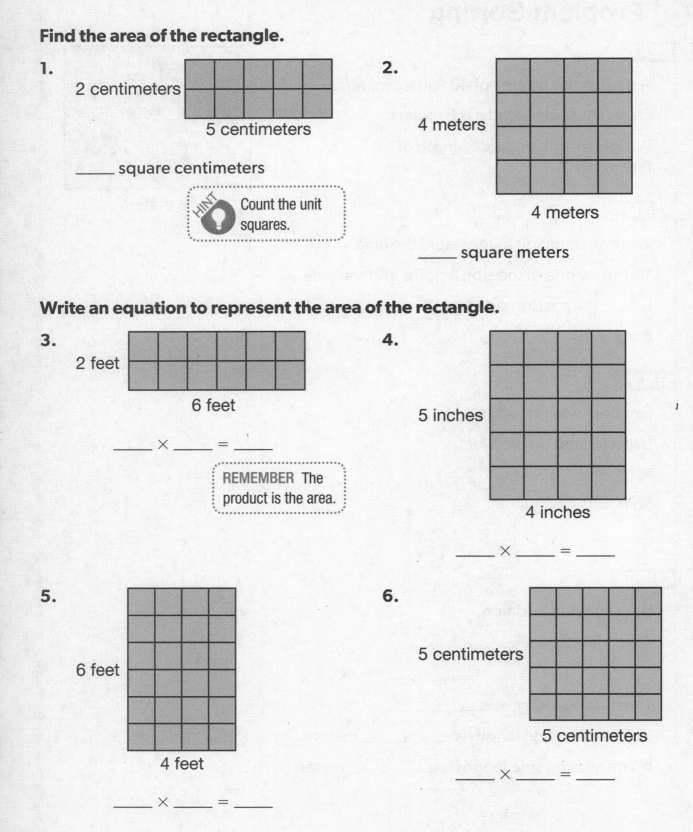

1.

2 centimeters

5 centimeters

_____ square centimeters

HINT Count the unit squares.

2.

4 meters

4 meters

_____ square meters

Write an equation to represent the area of the rectangle.

3.

2 feet

6 feet

_____ × _____ = _____

REMEMBER The product is the area.

4.

5 inches

4 inches

_____ × _____ = _____

5.

6 feet

4 feet

_____ × _____ = _____

6.

5 centimeters

5 centimeters

_____ × _____ = _____

Find the area of the rectangle.

7.

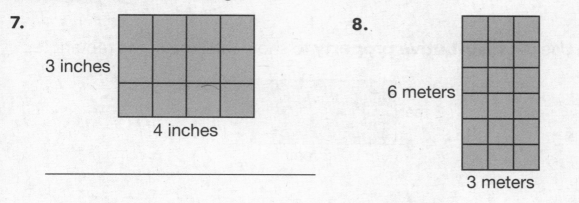

3 inches

4 inches

_____

8.

6 meters

3 meters

_____

Choose the best answer.

9. The side lengths of a card are 8 centimeters and 7 centimeters. What is the area of the card?

   A. 15 square centimeters

   B. 16 square centimeters

   C. 49 square centimeters

   D. 56 square centimeters

10. An office has side lengths of 9 feet. What is the area of the office?

    A. 9 square feet

    B. 18 square feet

    C. 81 square feet

    D. 99 square feet

Solve.

11. One of the side lengths of a sandbox is 6 feet. The area of the sandbox is 36 square feet. What is the other side length of the sandbox?

_____

12. **APPLY** Use the multiplication equation 5 × 6 = 30 to create an area word problem.

_____

_____

LESSON 25 Relating Area to Addition

EXAMPLE A Use the **distributive property** to show the area of the rectangle.

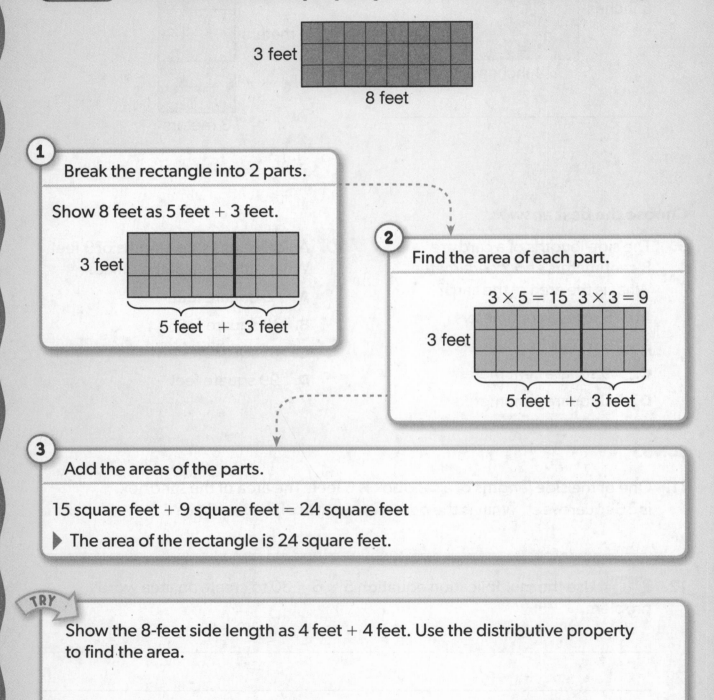

1 Break the rectangle into 2 parts.

Show 8 feet as 5 feet + 3 feet.

3 feet

5 feet + 3 feet

2 Find the area of each part.

$3 \times 5 = 15$ $3 \times 3 = 9$

3 feet

5 feet + 3 feet

3 Add the areas of the parts.

15 square feet + 9 square feet = 24 square feet

▶ The area of the rectangle is 24 square feet.

TRY

Show the 8-feet side length as 4 feet + 4 feet. Use the distributive property to find the area.

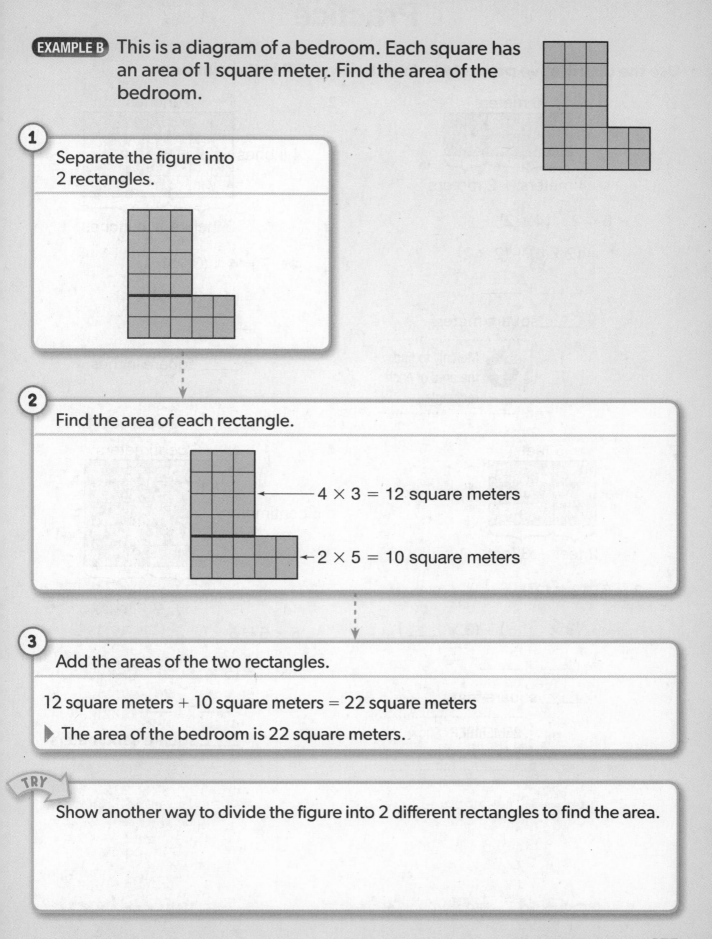

EXAMPLE B This is a diagram of a bedroom. Each square has an area of 1 square meter. Find the area of the bedroom.

1

Separate the figure into 2 rectangles.

2

Find the area of each rectangle.

$4 \times 3 = 12$ square meters

$2 \times 5 = 10$ square meters

3

Add the areas of the two rectangles.

12 square meters + 10 square meters = 22 square meters

▶ The area of the bedroom is 22 square meters.

TRY

Show another way to divide the figure into 2 different rectangles to find the area.

Practice

Use the distributive property to find the area. Fill in the numbers.

1.

6 meters

2 meters

4 meters + 2 meters

$2 \times 6 = 2 \times (4 + 2)$

$ = (2 \times 4) + (2 \times 2)$

$ = \underline{\hspace{1cm}} + \underline{\hspace{1cm}}$

$ = \underline{\hspace{1cm}}$ square meters

HINT Multiply to find the area of each rectangle.

2.

7 inches

4 inches

3 inches + 4 inches

$4 \times 7 = 4 \times (3 + 4)$

$ = (4 \times 3) + (4 \times 4)$

$ = \underline{\hspace{1cm}} + \underline{\hspace{1cm}}$

$ = \underline{\hspace{1cm}}$ square inches

3.

5 feet

3 feet

2 feet + 3 feet

$3 \times 5 = 3 \times (2 + \underline{\hspace{1cm}})$

$ = (3 \times \underline{\hspace{0.6cm}}) + (3 \times \underline{\hspace{0.6cm}})$

$ = \underline{\hspace{1cm}} + \underline{\hspace{1cm}}$

$ = \underline{\hspace{1cm}}$ square feet

REMEMBER Show 5 feet as a sum.

4.

6 centimeters

5 centimeters

3 centimeters + 3 centimeters

$5 \times 6 = 5 \times (\underline{\hspace{0.6cm}} + \underline{\hspace{0.6cm}})$

$ = (5 \times \underline{\hspace{0.6cm}}) + (5 \times \underline{\hspace{0.6cm}})$

$ = \underline{\hspace{1cm}} + \underline{\hspace{1cm}}$

$ = \underline{\hspace{1cm}}$ square centimeters

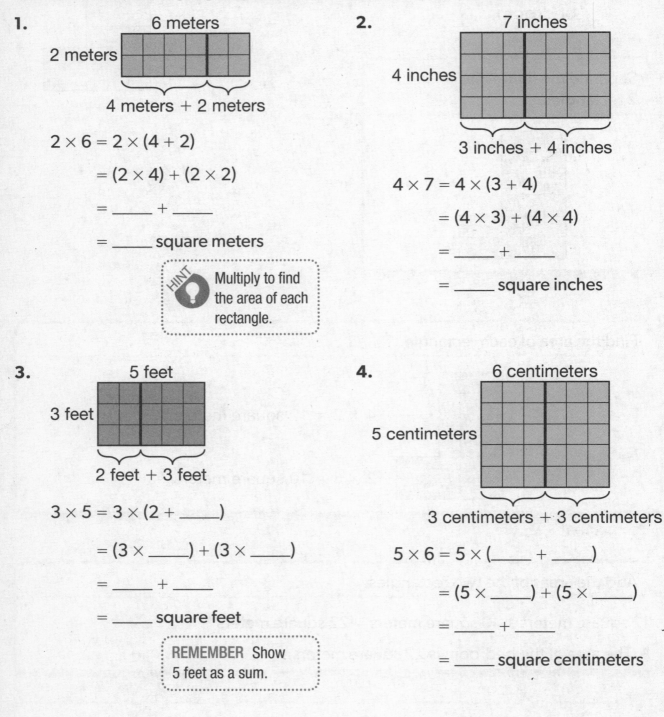

Separate the figure into 2 rectangles. Label one Rectangle A and the other Rectangle B. Find the area of each rectangle. Then add the areas to find the area of the whole figure.

5. Area of Rectangle A: _____ square units

    Area of Rectangle B: _____ square units

    Area of Figure: _____ square units

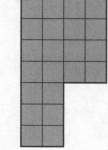

6. Area of Rectangle A: _____ square units

    Area of Rectangle B: _____ square units

    Area of Figure: _____ square units

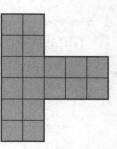

Solve.

7. To the right is a diagram of an office. Each square has an area of 1 square foot. Show how you can divide the office into 2 rectangles. Then find the area of the office.

    _____

    _____

8. **DEMONSTRATE** Use the distributive property to find the area of the rectangle.

    _____

    _____

    4 meters

    9 meters

9. **CREATE** On the grid to the right, draw a figure that can be separated into 2 rectangles. Then give the figure to a classmate to find its area by separating it into 2 rectangles.

    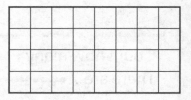

Perimeter

UNDERSTAND The distance around a figure is the **perimeter**.
Use ●————— to find the perimeter of the figure.

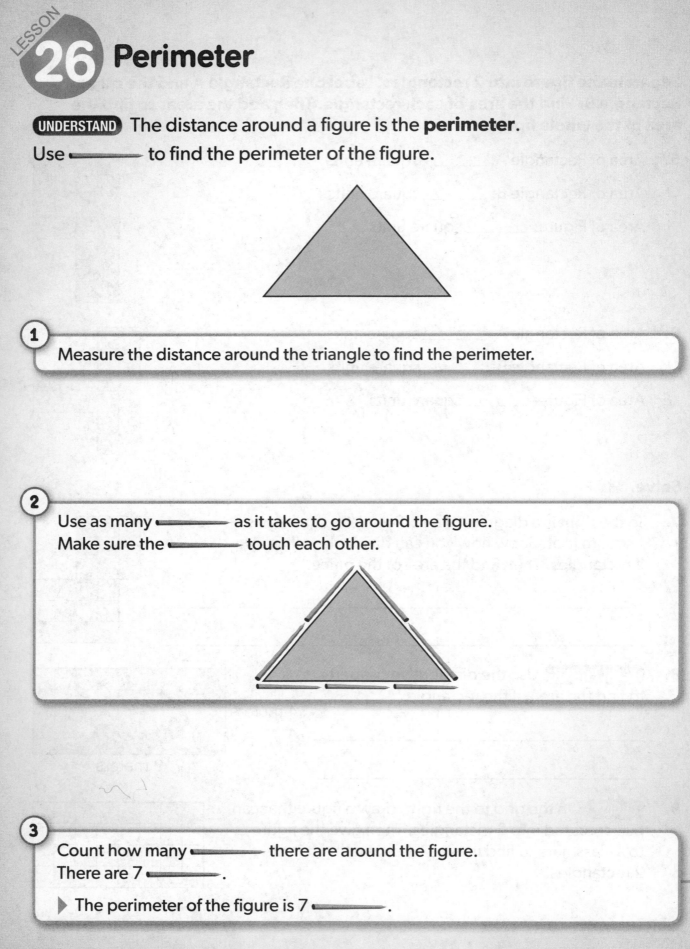

1 Measure the distance around the triangle to find the perimeter.

2 Use as many ●————— as it takes to go around the figure.
Make sure the ●————— touch each other.

3 Count how many ●————— there are around the figure.
There are 7 ●—————.

▶ The perimeter of the figure is 7 ●—————.

⊷ Connect

Find the perimeter of this figure.

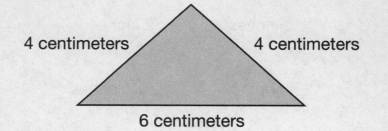

4 centimeters   4 centimeters

6 centimeters

1

Find the perimeter of the figure.

Measure the length of each side of the triangle.

2

Look at the side lengths.

Two sides are each 4 centimeters long.
One side is 6 centimeters long.

3

Add the side lengths.

4 centimeters + 4 centimeters + 6 centimeters = 14 centimeters

▶ The perimeter of the figure is 14 centimeters.

TRY

The side lengths of a triangle are 8 inches, 8 inches, and 10 inches. What is the perimeter of the triangle?

EXAMPLE A What is the perimeter of this figure?

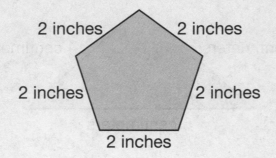

2 inches 2 inches

2 inches 2 inches

2 inches

1

Look at the side lengths.

All sides are the same length.

Each side is 2 inches long.

2

Use multiplication.

All 5 sides are 2 inches long.

5 × 2 inches = 10 inches

▶ The perimeter of the figure is 10 inches.

CHECK

Use repeated addition to check multiplication.

_____ + _____ + _____ + _____ + _____ = _____ inches

EXAMPLE B This figure has a perimeter of 24 meters.
What is the missing side length?

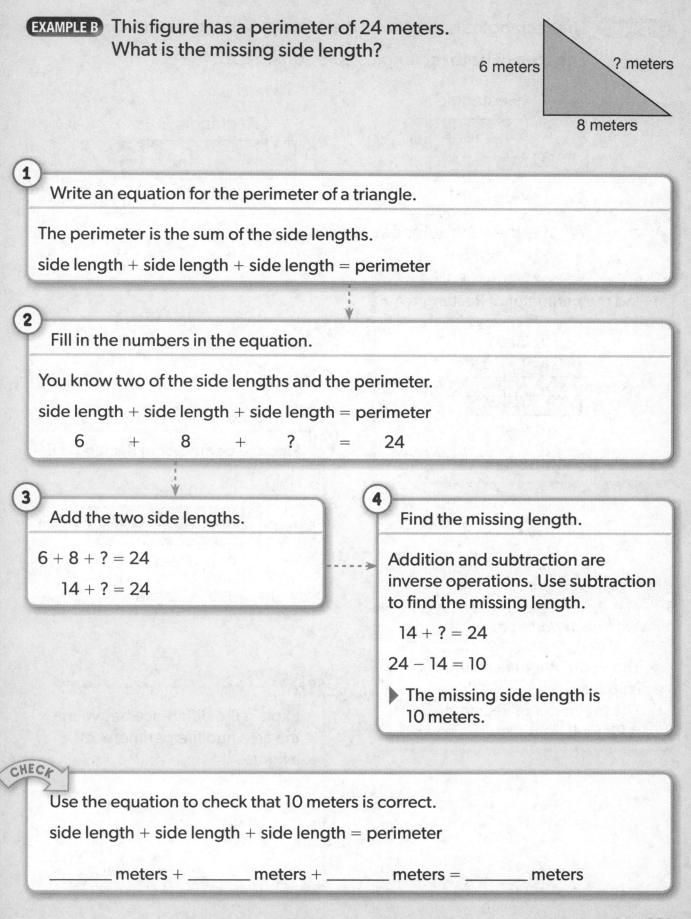

6 meters   ? meters

8 meters

1

Write an equation for the perimeter of a triangle.

The perimeter is the sum of the side lengths.

side length + side length + side length = perimeter

2

Fill in the numbers in the equation.

You know two of the side lengths and the perimeter.

side length + side length + side length = perimeter

6   +   8   +   ?   =   24

3

Add the two side lengths.

6 + 8 + ? = 24

14 + ? = 24

4

Find the missing length.

Addition and subtraction are inverse operations. Use subtraction to find the missing length.

14 + ? = 24

24 − 14 = 10

▶ The missing side length is 10 meters.

CHECK

Use the equation to check that 10 meters is correct.

side length + side length + side length = perimeter

_____ meters + _____ meters + _____ meters = _____ meters

EXAMPLE C The rectangles below have the same area but different perimeters. The area of both rectangles is 18 square feet.

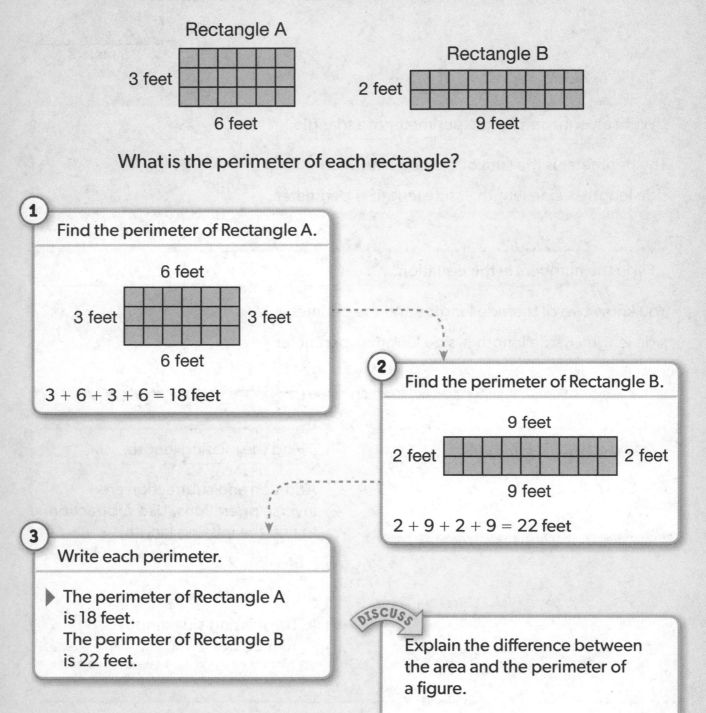

Rectangle A

3 feet

6 feet

Rectangle B

2 feet

9 feet

What is the perimeter of each rectangle?

1

Find the perimeter of Rectangle A.

6 feet

3 feet   3 feet

6 feet

3 + 6 + 3 + 6 = 18 feet

2

Find the perimeter of Rectangle B.

9 feet

2 feet   2 feet

9 feet

2 + 9 + 2 + 9 = 22 feet

3

Write each perimeter.

▶ The perimeter of Rectangle A is 18 feet.
The perimeter of Rectangle B is 22 feet.

DISCUSS

Explain the difference between the area and the perimeter of a figure.

⚙️ Problem Solving

READ

Emily wants to put a fence around her vegetable garden. Fencing costs $8 a foot. How much will it cost Emily to buy the fencing?

17 feet

12 feet   12 feet

17 feet

PLAN

Step 1: Find the perimeter of her garden.

Step 2: Multiply the perimeter by $8 to find the cost of the fencing.

SOLVE

Step 1: Add the side lengths to find the perimeter of her garden.

side length + side length + side length + side length = _____?_____ feet

$17 + 12 + 17 + 12 = $ _____ feet

Step 2: Multiply the perimeter by $8 to find the cost.

$58 \times \$8 = $ _____

CHECK

You can estimate to decide if your answer is reasonable.

Step 1: Round the side lengths to the nearest ten. Then add.

$$17 + 12 + 17 + 12$$
$$\downarrow \quad \downarrow \quad \downarrow \quad \downarrow$$
$$20 + 10 + 20 + 10 = \underline{\hspace{1.5cm}} \text{ feet}$$

Step 2: Multiply the estimated perimeter by $8.

$$60 \times \$8 = \$480$$

Since _____ is close to $480, the answer is reasonable.

▶ It will cost Emily _____ to buy the fencing.

Practice

Find the perimeter of the figure. Write a number sentence.

1.

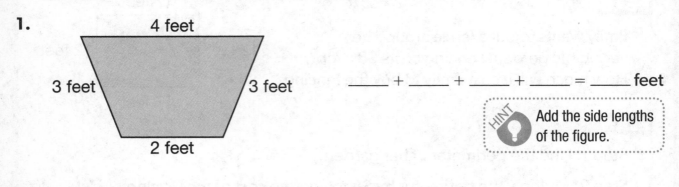

_____ + _____ + _____ + _____ = _____ feet

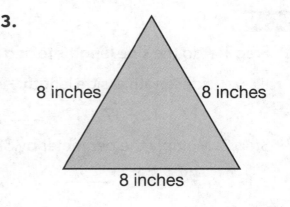

HINT Add the side lengths of the figure.

Find the perimeter of each figure.

2.

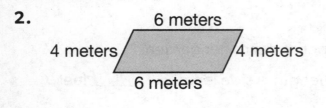

_____

3.

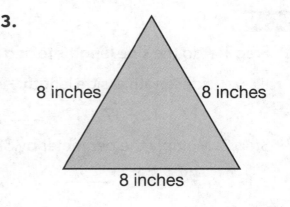

_____

Find the missing side length.

4. Perimeter = 20 feet

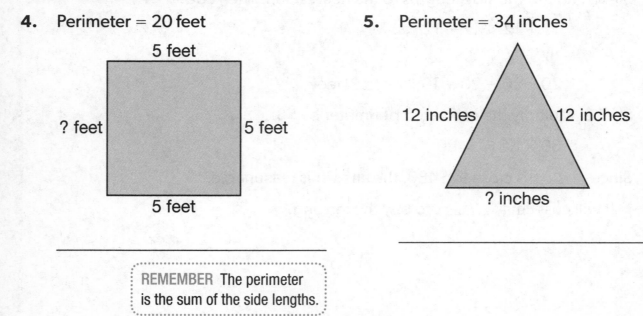

_____

REMEMBER The perimeter is the sum of the side lengths.

5. Perimeter = 34 inches

_____

Choose the best answer.

6. Each side of a square is 7 centimeters long. Which equation can you use to find the perimeter?

   A. $4 + 7 + 4 + 7 = \Box$

   B. $4 + 4 + 4 + 4 = \Box$

   C. $7 \times 7 = \Box$

   D. $4 \times 7 = \Box$

7. A piece of paper has side lengths of 11 inches and 8 inches. What is the perimeter of the piece of paper?

   A. 19 inches

   B. 30 inches

   C. 38 inches

   D. 88 inches

Solve.

8. Hank has a triangular rug in his bedroom. The perimeter of the rug is 14 feet. Two of the side lengths are 6 feet. What is the length of the third side of the rug?

_____

9. A square dance floor has a perimeter of 32 meters. What is the length of each side of the dance floor?

_____

10. (ILLUSTRATE) To the right is a diagram of a closet floor. It has an area of 24 square feet and a perimeter of 20 feet. Draw and label a rectangle with the same area but a different perimeter. Draw and label another rectangle with the same perimeter but a different area.

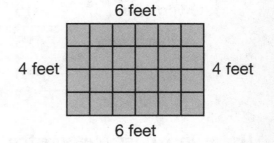

6 feet

4 feet   4 feet

6 feet

4 Review

Write the time shown on the clock.

1.

2.

3.

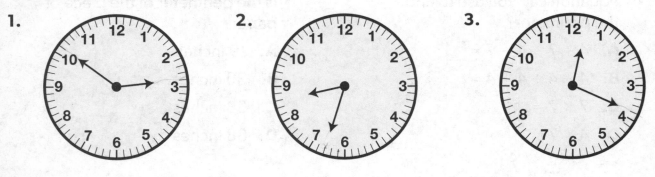

_____   _____   _____

Complete the picture graph to match the data in the table.

4.   **Time Spent Reading**

Student	Number of Minutes
Heath	20
Owen	15
Jasmine	25
Patsy	30

Time Spent Reading

Heath	
Owen	
Jasmine	
Patsy	

Key: Each ▲ = 5 minutes

Use an inch ruler. Measure the length to the nearest $\frac{1}{4}$ inch.

5.

6.

_____   _____

Complete the graph to match the data in the table.

7.

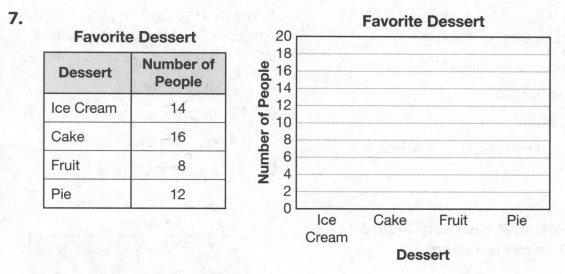

Favorite Dessert

Dessert	Number of People
Ice Cream	14
Cake	16
Fruit	8
Pie	12

Use the graph in question 7 to answer questions 8–11.

8. How many people chose pie as their favorite dessert?

_____

9. How many people in all were asked about their favorite dessert? Show your work.

_____

10. How many more people like ice cream than like fruit as their favorite dessert? Show your work.

_____

11. Which two desserts did a total of 20 people choose as their favorite dessert? Show your work.

_____

Find the area of the figure.

12.

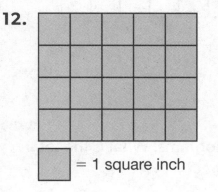

☐ = 1 square inch

_____

13.

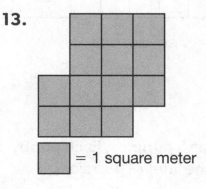

☐ = 1 square meter

_____

Choose the best answer.

14. A rug is 9 feet long and 6 feet wide. What is the area of the rug?

   A. 15 square feet

   B. 30 square feet

   C. 45 square feet

   D. 54 square feet

15. Adam made a painting that has side lengths of 4 meters and 3 meters. What is the area of Adam's painting?

   A. 7 square meters

   B. 12 square meters

   C. 14 square meters

   D. 28 square meters

Use the distributive property to find the area. Fill in the numbers.

16. $3 \times 6 = 3 \times (3 + 3)$

      $= (3 \times 3) + (3 \times 3)$

      $=$ _____ $+$ _____

      $=$ _____ square inches

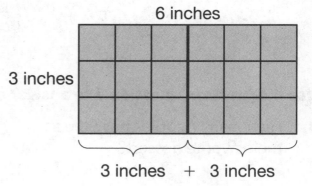

17. ILLUSTRATE Draw 2 rectangles with the same area but different perimeters on the grid below. Label each rectangle with the area and the perimeter.

☐ = 1 square unit

Solve.

18. A litter has 6 puppies. Each puppy has a mass of 2 kilograms. What is the total mass of the litter of puppies?

_____

How Long Is Your Shoe?

How Long Is Your Shoe?

How Long Is Your Shoe?

You will need an inch ruler for this task.

Measure the right shoe of 15 classmates. Measure the length to the nearest $\frac{1}{2}$ inch. List the measurements in the table below.

Shoe Lengths (in inches)

Use the measurements to make a line plot. Make sure to label the number line.

Shoe Lengths

$\longleftrightarrow$

1. What is the length of the longest shoe? _____

2. How many classmates have the longest shoe? _____

3. Use the data in the line plot to create a problem. Give it to a classmate to solve.

    _____

    _____

Grade 2	Grade 3	Grade 4

Grade 4 MD

Solve problems involving measurement and conversion of measurements from a larger unit to a smaller unit.

Grade 2 G

Reason with shapes and their attributes.

Grade 3 G

Reason with shapes and their attributes.

Grade 4 G

Draw and identify lines and angles, and classify shapes by properties of their lines and angles.

Domain 5
Geometry

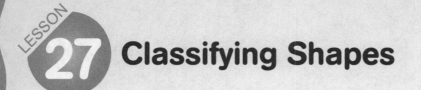

LESSON 27 · Classifying Shapes

EXAMPLE A Which of the shapes shown below are **polygons**?

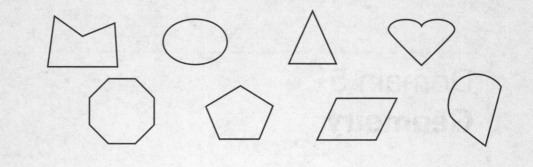

1 Look at the sides of the shapes.

A polygon is a closed shape with straight sides.

2 Sort the shapes into two groups.

The shapes with straight sides are polygons.

The shapes with curved sides are not polygons.

Polygons

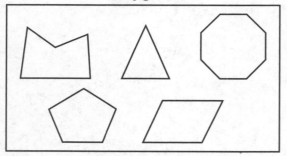

Not Polygons

▶ The shapes are sorted above.

MODEL

Draw a shape that is not a polygon.

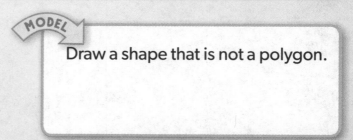

EXAMPLE B This shape can be described as a polygon, a **quadrilateral**, and a rectangle.

Draw a shape that is a polygon and a quadrilateral, but not a rectangle.

1 Think about a polygon.

A polygon is a closed shape with straight sides.

2 Think about a quadrilateral.

A quadrilateral is a polygon with 4 sides and 4 **angles**.

3 Think about a rectangle.

A rectangle is a quadrilateral with 4 square corners.

4 Draw a polygon that is a quadrilateral, but not a rectangle.

The shape should have 4 straight sides but should not have 4 square corners.

▶ The shape above is a polygon and a quadrilateral, but it is not a rectangle.

TRY

Draw a different quadrilateral that is not a rectangle.

Practice

Is the shape a polygon? Write _yes_ or _no_.

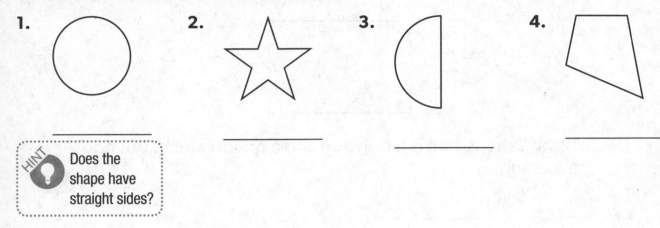

1.

2.

3.

4.

HINT Does the shape have straight sides?

Complete the table.

	Shape	Picture	Number of Sides	Number of Angles
5.	triangle		3	
6.	pentagon			5
7.	hexagon			
8.	octagon			

Write all the names from this list that describe the shape.

| quadrilateral | rectangle | square | rhombus |

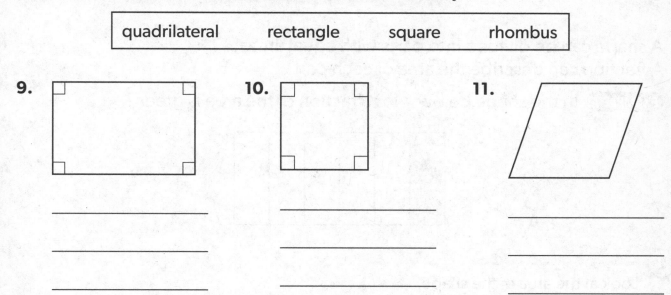

9. _____

_____

_____

10. _____

_____

_____

11. _____

_____

_____

Choose the best answer.

12. Which word best describes this shape?

A. triangle

B. quadrilateral

C. square

D. pentagon

13. Which word does **not** describe this shape?

A. polygon

B. quadrilateral

C. rhombus

D. square

Solve.

14. Carrie drew a polygon with 5 straight sides and 5 angles. What polygon did Carrie draw?

_____

15. **CONCLUDE** Explain why all squares are rhombuses, but not all rhombuses are squares.

_____

_____

A shape can be divided into parts with equal areas.
A fraction can describe the area of each part.

EXAMPLE A In the shape below, what fraction of the area is green?

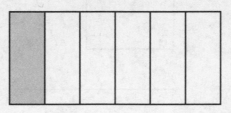

1

Look at the area of the shape.

The area of the shape is the whole rectangle.

2

Look at the parts of the shape.

The shape is divided into 6 equal parts.

Each part is $\frac{1}{6}$ of the whole shape.

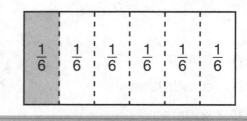

3

Find the area of the shape that is green.

One part of the shape is green.

So the green part is $\frac{1}{6}$ of the area of the shape.

▶ $\frac{1}{6}$ of the area of the shape is green.

DISCUSS

Explain how a fraction relates to a part of the area of a shape.

EXAMPLE B In the shape below, what fraction of the area is green?

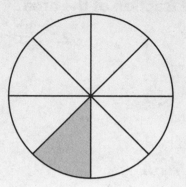

1

Look at the area of the shape.

The area of the shape is the whole circle.

2

Look at the parts of the shape.

The shape is divided into 8 equal parts.

Each part is $\frac{1}{8}$ of the whole shape.

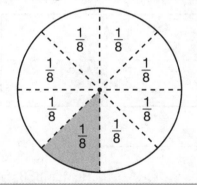

3

Find the area of the shape that is green.

One part of the shape is green.

So the green part is $\frac{1}{8}$ of the area of the circle.

▶ $\frac{1}{8}$ of the area of the shape is green.

TRY

If two parts of the shape are green, what fraction of the area of the shape is green?

Practice

Shade the shape to show the fraction of the area.

1. $\frac{1}{4}$ of the area

2. $\frac{1}{3}$ of the area

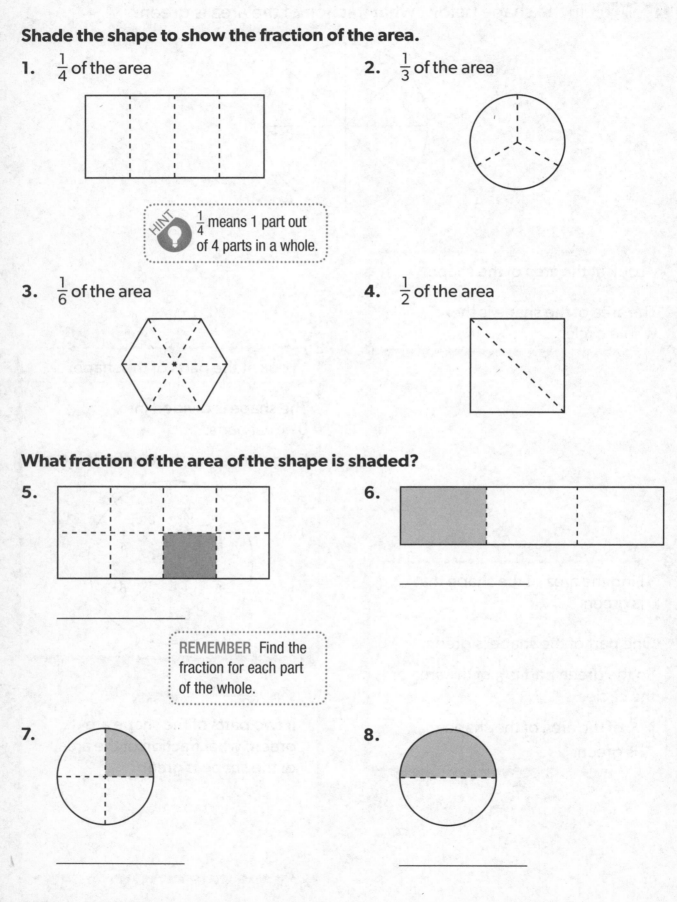

HINT $\frac{1}{4}$ means 1 part out of 4 parts in a whole.

3. $\frac{1}{6}$ of the area

4. $\frac{1}{2}$ of the area

What fraction of the area of the shape is shaded?

5.

6.

_____

REMEMBER Find the fraction for each part of the whole.

7.

8.

_____   _____

Use the shape for each question.

9. Divide the shape into 3 parts with equal areas. Color $\frac{1}{3}$ of the area of the shape green.

10. Divide the shape into 6 parts with equal areas. Color $\frac{1}{6}$ of the area of the shape yellow.

Choose the best answer.

11. Which diagram shows $\frac{1}{4}$ of the area of the shape is blue?

A.
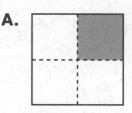

B.
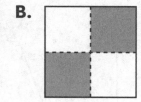

C.
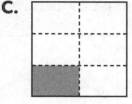

D.
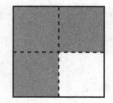

Solve.

12. Monica has a rug in her bedroom. What fraction of the area of the rug is white?

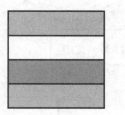

_____

13. This tabletop is made with different color tiles. What fraction of the area of the tabletop is green?

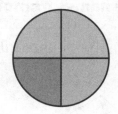

_____

14. (CONCLUDE) When you use a fraction to describe parts of the area of a shape, why is it important for the parts to be equal?

_____

_____

Draw a line from each object to the name of the polygon with the same shape.

1.

hexagon   triangle   quadrilateral   octagon   pentagon

Draw a line from each shape to its name.

2.

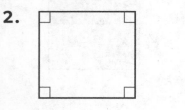 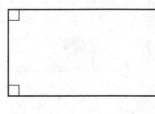 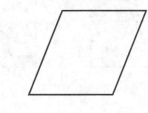

rectangle   square   rhombus

Write all the names from this list that describe the shape.

quadrilateral	rectangle	polygon

3.

_____

_____

4.

_____

_____

5.

_____

_____

Choose the best answer.

6. What is the name of this shape?

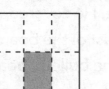

    A. octagon

    B. hexagon

    C. pentagon

    D. quadrilateral

7. What is the name of this shape?

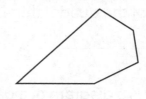

    A. triangle

    B. quadrilateral

    C. pentagon

    D. hexagon

What fraction of the area of the shape is shaded?

8.

9.

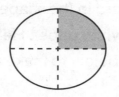

10.

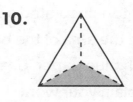

_____ _____ _____

11. Divide the shape into 4 parts with equal areas. Color $\frac{1}{4}$ of the area of the shape yellow.

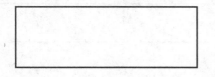

12. Divide the shape into 8 parts with equal areas. Color $\frac{1}{8}$ of the area of the shape blue.

Solve.

13. Jason drew a quadrilateral with 4 equal sides and 4 square corners. What is the name of the quadrilateral that Jason drew?

    _____

14. Below is a diagram of a parking lot. It is divided into equal areas for different types of vehicles. What fraction of the area of the parking lot is for trucks?

    _____

15. Ashton decorated a bulletin board in the shape of a rectangle. He covered $\frac{1}{6}$ of the area of the board with white paper. He covered the rest of the board with blue paper. Use the space below to make a diagram of the bulletin board. Explain your work.

    _____

    _____

    _____

16. **ILLUSTRATE** Draw a quadrilateral that is **not** a rectangle.

17. **ILLUSTRATE** Draw a quadrilateral that is **not** a rhombus.

SORTING SHAPES

Sort the shapes into two groups by drawing each shape in the correct box below.

1.

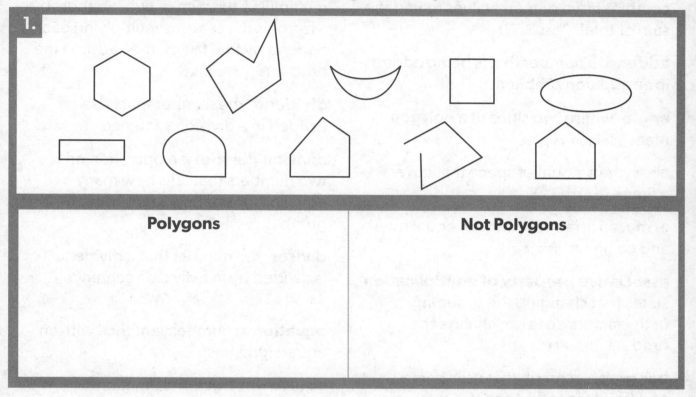

Polygons	Not Polygons

Sort the shapes into two groups by drawing each shape in the correct box below.

2.

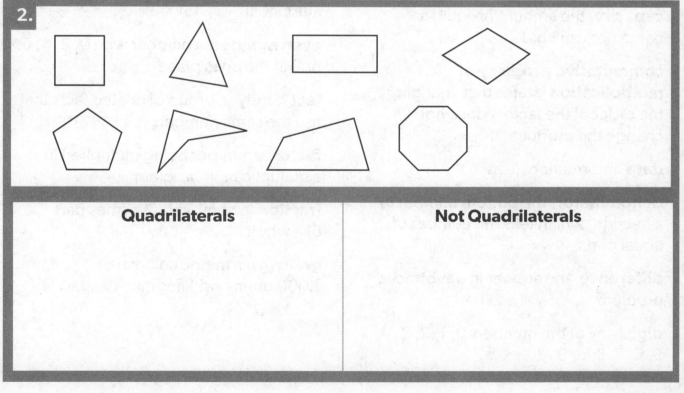

Quadrilaterals	Not Quadrilaterals

Glossary

addition (add) an operation that combines two or more values to find the sum or total (Lesson 11)

addend a number that is being added in an addition problem (Lesson 6)

angle where two sides of a polygon meet (Lesson 27)

area the amount of space that covers a figure (Lesson 23)

array an arrangement with equal rows and columns (Lesson 3)

associative property of multiplication states that changing the grouping of the factors does not change the product (Lesson 6)

bar graph a graph that uses bars of different lengths to represent data (Lesson 20)

capacity the amount of liquid a container can hold (Lesson 18)

commutative property of multiplication states that changing the order of the factors does not change the product (Lesson 6)

data information (Lesson 19)

denominator the bottom number in a fraction, which tells the number of equal parts (Lesson 13)

difference the answer in a subtraction problem (Lessons 8 and 11)

digit any of the numbers 0, 1, 2, 3, 4, 5, 6, 7, 8, or 9 (Lesson 10)

distributive property states that multiplying the sum of two numbers by a factor is the same as multiplying each addend by that factor, then adding the products (Lessons 6, 25)

dividend the number that is being divided in a division sentence (Lesson 2)

division (divide) an operation on two numbers that tells how many equal groups or how many in each group (Lesson 2)

divisor the number that a dividend is divided by in a division sentence (Lesson 2)

equation a number sentence with an equal sign (Lesson 3)

equivalent fractions fractions that have different numerators and denominators but name the same amount (Lesson 15)

even number a number with 0, 2, 4, 6, or 8 in the ones place (Lesson 9)

fact family a group of related facts that use the same numbers (Lesson 5)

factor a number being multiplied in a multiplication problem (Lesson 1)

fraction a number that names part of a whole (Lesson 13)

gram (g) a metric unit of mass; 1,000 grams = 1 kilogram (Lesson 18)

hour (h) a unit of time; 1 hour = 60 minutes (Lesson 17)

inch (in.) a customary unit of length; 12 inches = 1 foot (Lesson 21)

inch ruler a tool used to measure length (Lesson 21)

inverse operation an operation that undoes another operation; addition and subtraction are inverse operations; multiplication and division are inverse operations (Lessons 5, 11)

key (in a picture graph) tells how many each symbol represents (Lesson 19)

kilogram (kg) a metric unit of mass; 1 kilogram = 1,000 grams (Lesson 18)

length the measure of how long, how wide, or how tall an object is (Lesson 21)

line plot a display that uses Xs above a number line to represent data (Lesson 22)

liquid volume the amount of liquid a container can hold (Lesson 18)

liter (L) a metric unit of capacity; 1 liter = 1,000 milliliters (Lesson 18)

mass the amount of matter in an object (Lesson 18)

milliliter (mL) a metric unit of capacity; 1,000 milliliters = 1 liter (Lesson 18)

minuend the number that is subtracted from in a subtraction problem (Lessons 8 and 11)

minute (min) a unit of time; 1 minute = 60 seconds (Lesson 17)

multiple a product of two numbers (Lesson 12)

multiplication (multiply) an operation that joins equal groups (Lesson 1)

number pattern a set of numbers that follows a rule (Lesson 9)

numerator the top number in a fraction (Lesson 13)

odd number a number with 1, 3, 5, 7, or 9 in the ones place (Lesson 9)

perimeter the distance around a figure (Lesson 26)

picture graph a graph that uses symbols to represent data (Lesson 19)

polygon a closed shape with three or more straight sides (Lesson 27)

product the answer in a multiplication problem (Lesson 1)

quadrilateral a polygon with 4 sides and 4 angles (Lesson 27)

quotient the answer in a division problem (Lesson 2)

rectangle a quadrilateral with 4 sides and 4 square corners (Lesson 23)

regroup to rename a number by exchanging amounts of equal value (Lesson 11)

repeated addition adding the same number multiple times (Lesson 3)

repeated subtraction subtracting the same number multiple times (Lesson 4)

round a way to estimate numbers (Lesson 10)

scale (in a bar graph) gives the value of each bar in the graph (Lesson 20)

square unit a square that has a side length of 1 unit (Lesson 23)

subtraction (subtract) an operation that takes a value away from another value to find the difference (Lesson 11)

subtrahend the number that is subtracted in a subtraction sentence (Lessons 8 and 11)

sum the answer in an addition problem (Lessons 8 and 11)

Math Tool: Properties of Multiplication

Associative Property of Multiplication

The grouping of the factors does not change the product.

$(2 \times 5) \times 4 = 2 \times (5 \times 4)$

$10 \times 4 = 2 \times 20$

$40 = 40$

$(1 \times 5) \times 6 = 1 \times (5 \times 6)$

$5 \times 6 = 1 \times 30$

$30 = 30$

Commutative Property of Multiplication

The order of the factors does not change the product.

$5 \times 6 = 6 \times 5$

$30 = 30$

$4 \times 9 = 9 \times 4$

$36 = 36$

Identity Property of 1

Any number multiplied by 1 is that number.

$8 \times 1 = 8$

$1 \times 10 = 10$

Distributive Property of Multiplication

Multiplying the sum of two numbers by a factor is the same as multiplying each addend by the factor and adding the products.

$$8 \times 9 = 8 \times (5 + 4)$$
$$= (8 \times 5) + (8 \times 4)$$
$$= 40 + 32$$
$$= 72$$
$$8 \times 9 = 72$$

Math Tool: Addition Table

+	0	1	2	3	4	5	6	7	8	9	10
0	0	1	2	3	4	5	6	7	8	9	10
1	1	2	3	4	5	6	7	8	9	10	11
2	2	3	4	5	6	7	8	9	10	11	12
3	3	4	5	6	7	8	9	10	11	12	13
4	4	5	6	7	8	9	10	11	12	13	14
5	5	6	7	8	9	10	11	12	13	14	15
6	6	7	8	9	10	11	12	13	14	15	16
7	7	8	9	10	11	12	13	14	15	16	17
8	8	9	10	11	12	13	14	15	16	17	18
9	9	10	11	12	13	14	15	16	17	18	19
10	10	11	12	13	14	15	16	17	18	19	20

Math Tool: Multiplication Table

×	0	1	2	3	4	5	6	7	8	9	10
0	0	0	0	0	0	0	0	0	0	0	0
1	0	1	2	3	4	5	6	7	8	9	10
2	0	2	4	6	8	10	12	14	16	18	20
3	0	3	6	9	12	15	18	21	24	27	30
4	0	4	8	12	16	20	24	28	32	36	40
5	0	5	10	15	20	25	30	35	40	45	50
6	0	6	12	18	24	30	36	42	48	54	60
7	0	7	14	21	28	35	42	49	56	63	70
8	0	8	16	24	32	40	48	56	64	72	80
9	0	9	18	27	36	45	54	63	72	81	90
10	0	10	20	30	40	50	60	70	80	90	100

Math Tool: Place-Value Tables

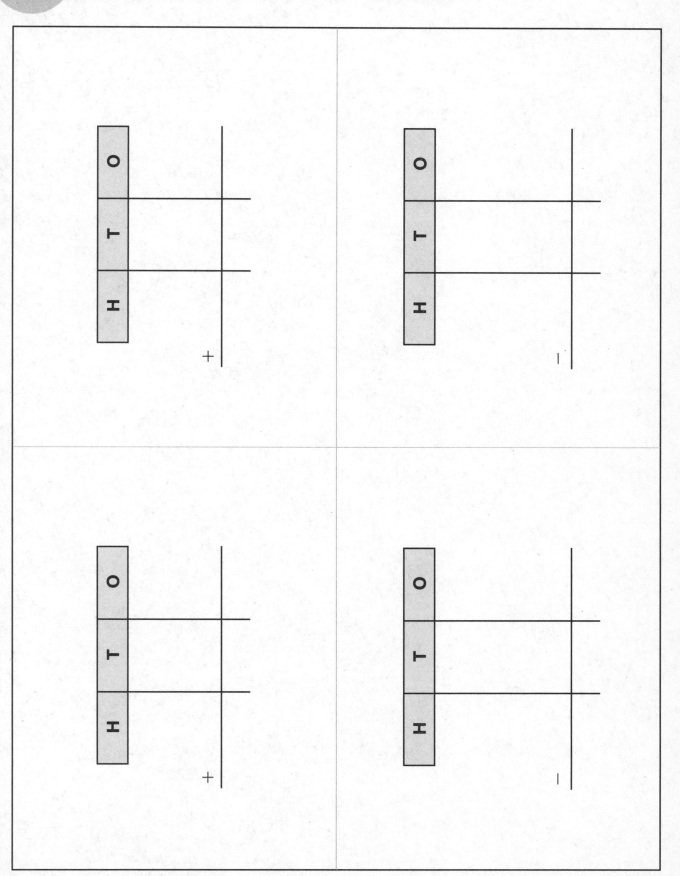

Math Tool: Place-Value Models

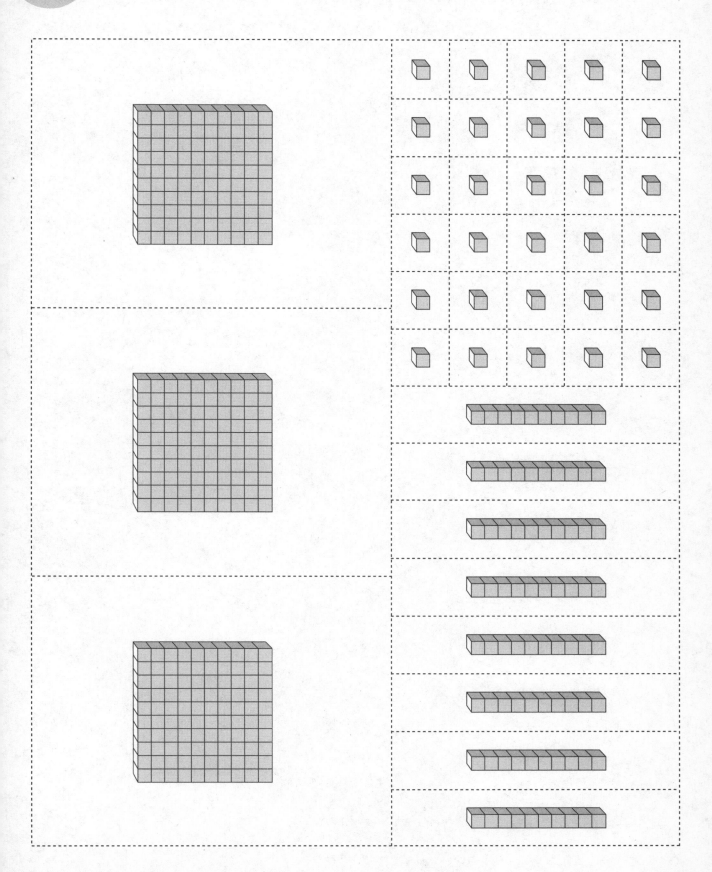

Math Tool: Number Lines

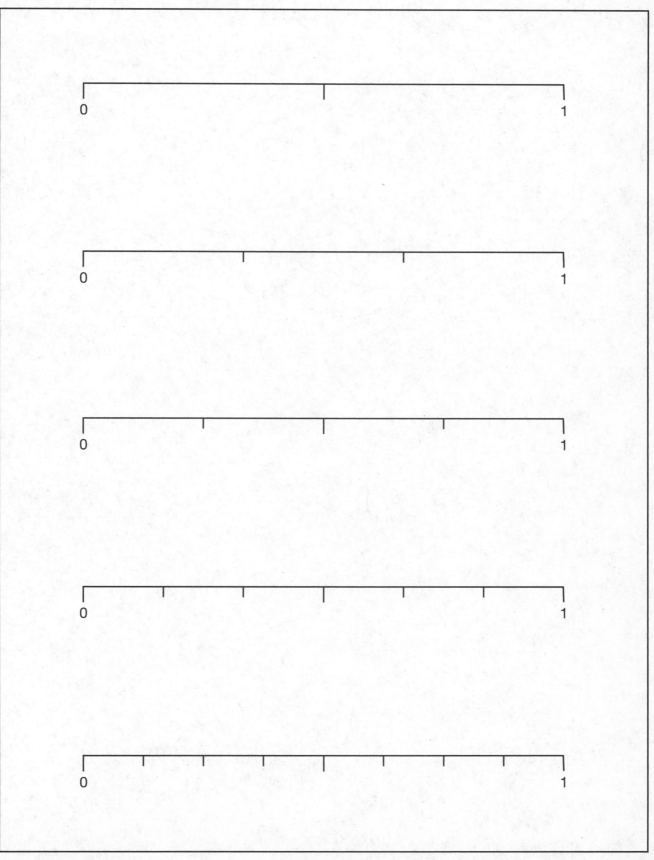

Math Tool: Fraction Strips

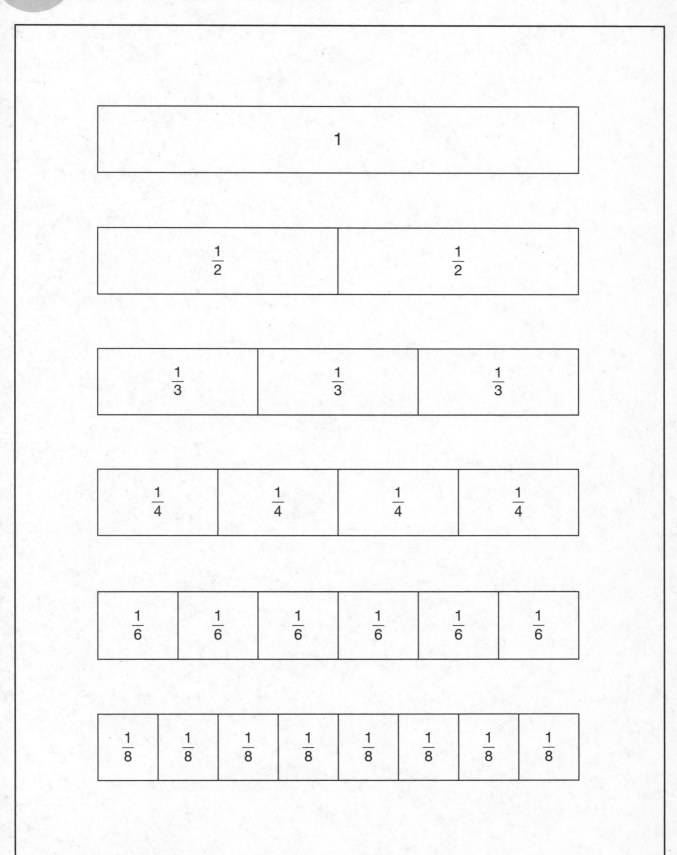

Math Tool: Two-Dimensional Shapes

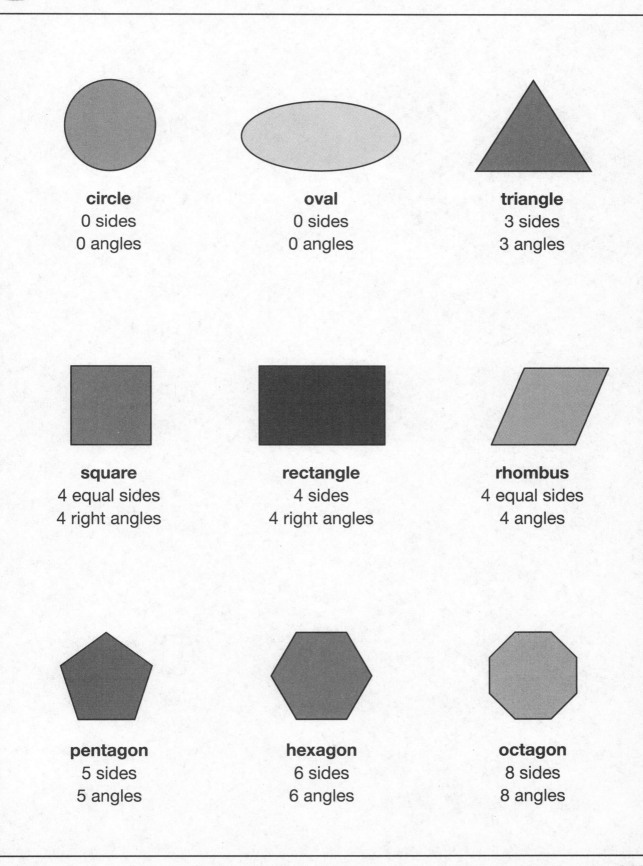

circle
0 sides
0 angles

oval
0 sides
0 angles

triangle
3 sides
3 angles

square
4 equal sides
4 right angles

rectangle
4 sides
4 right angles

rhombus
4 equal sides
4 angles

pentagon
5 sides
5 angles

hexagon
6 sides
6 angles

octagon
8 sides
8 angles

Notes

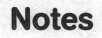

Notes

Notes